AMERICAN POLITICAL, ECONOMIC AND SECURITY ISSUES SERIES

CLOSING GUANTANAMO – ISSUES AND LEGAL MATTERS SURROUNDING THE DETENTION CENTER'S END

AMERICAN POLITICAL, ECONOMIC, AND SECURITY ISSUES SERIES

Call for A New Era in the U.S. Budget
Benjamin J. Walters (Editor)
2010. ISBN: 978-1-60741-883-2

Call for A New Era in the U.S. Budget
Benjamin J. Walters (Editor)
2010. ISBN: 978-1-61668-778-6 (Online Book)

War at Any Price - Economic Costs Beyond the Federal Budget
William J. Butler (Editor)
2010. ISBN: 978-1-60741-441-40.

Closing Guantanamo - Issues and Legal Matters Surrounding the Detention Centers End
Noah M. Claeys (Editor)
2010. ISBN: 978-1-60741-511-4

The Land and Maritime Boundary Disputes of the Americas
Rongxing Guo
2009. ISBN: 978-1-60741-636-4

Federal Spending: A Riddle Wrapped up in an Enigma
Frederick C. Hargis
2010. ISBN: 978-1-60741-728-6

The Joint Operating Environment 2008: Using History to Inform the Future
Michaël Peeters (Editor)
2010. ISBN: 978-1-60876-035-0

Foreign Investment In U.S. Securities
Declan J. Byrne (Editor)
2010. ISBN: 978-1-60876-084-8

The State Secrets Privilege and Other Limits on Classified Information
Jonathon W. Collingsworth (Editor)
2010. ISBN: 978-1-60876-967-4

The State Secrets Privilege and Other Limits on Classified Information
Jonathon W. Collingsworth (Editor)
2010. ISBN: 978-1-60876-430-3 (Online Book)

AMERICAN POLITICAL, ECONOMIC AND SECURITY ISSUES SERIES

CLOSING GUANTANAMO – ISSUES AND LEGAL MATTERS SURROUNDING THE DETENTION CENTER'S END

NOAH M. CLAEYS
EDITOR

Nova Science Publishers, Inc.
New York

For permission to use material from this book please contact us:
Telephone 631-231-7269; Fax 631-231-8175
Web Site: http://www.novapublishers.com

LIBRARY OF CONGRESS CATALOGING-IN-PUBLICATION DATA

Closing Guantanamo : issues and legal matters surrounding the detention centers end / editor, Noah M. Claeys.
p. cm.
Includes index.
ISBN 978-1-60741-511-4 (hardcover)
1. Detention of persons--Cuba--Guantánamo Bay Naval Base. 2. Guantánamo Bay Detention Camp. 3. Prisoners of war--Legal status, laws, etc.--Cuba--Guantánamo Bay Naval Base. 4. Combatants and noncombatants (International law) 5. War on Terrorism, 2001---Law and legislation--United States. 6. Habeas corpus--United States. I. Claeys, Noah M.
KZ6496.C56 2009
343.73'01571--dc22

2009036563

ISBN: 978-1-60741-511-4

Published by Nova Science Publishers, Inc. ✦ New York

CONTENTS

PREFACE

This book provides an overview of major legal issues likely to arise as a result of executive and legislative action to close the Guantanamo detention facility. It discusses legal issues related to the transfer or release of Guantanamo detainees (either to a foreign country or into the U.S.), the continued detention of such persons in the U.S., and the possible removal of persons brought to the U.S. This book also discusses selected constitutional issues that may arise in the criminal prosecution of detainees, emphasizing the procedural and substantive protections that are utilized in different adjudicatory forums. Other issues discussed include detainees' right to a speedy trial, the prohibition against prosecution under ex post facto laws, and limitations upon the admissibility of hearsay and secret evidence in criminal cases. This book consists of public domain documents which have been located, gathered, combined, reformatted, and enhanced with a subject index, selectively edited and bound to provide easy access.

Chapter 1 - Following the terrorist attacks of 9/11, Congress passed the Authorization to Use Military Force (AUMF), which granted the President the authority "to use all necessary and appropriate force against those ... [who] planned, authorized, committed, or aided the terrorist attacks" against the United States." As part of the subsequent "war on terror," many persons captured during military operations in Afghanistan and elsewhere were transferred to the U.S. Naval Station at Guantanamo Bay, Cuba for detention and possible prosecution before military tribunals. Although nearly 800 persons have been transferred to Guantanamo since early 2002, the substantial majority of Guantanamo detainees have ultimately been transferred to a third country for continued detention or release. The roughly 250 detainees who remain fall into three categories: (1) persons placed in non-penal, preventative detention to stop them from rejoining hostilities; (2) persons who have been brought, or are expected to be brought, before a military tribunal to face criminal charges for alleged war crimes; and (3) persons who have been cleared for transfer or release to a third country, whom the United States continues to detain pending transfer. Although the Supreme Court ruled in *Boumediene v. Bush* that Guantanamo detainees may seek *habeas corpus* review of the legality of their detention, several legal issues remain unsettled, including the scope of *habeas* review available to Guantanamo detainees, the remedy available for those persons found to be unlawfully held by the United States, and the extent to which other constitutional provisions extend to noncitizens held at Guantanamo.

On January 22, 2009, President Barack Obama issued an Executive Order requiring the Guantanamo detention facility to be closed as soon as practicable, and no later than a year from the date of the Order. Officials in the Obama Administration have stated that the Administration will work with Congress to craft legislation to effectuate the facility's closure and clarify the legal status of detainees transferred to the United States.

The closure of the Guantanamo detention facility may raise a number of legal issues with respect to the individuals formerly interned there, particularly if those detainees are transferred to the United States. The nature and scope of constitutional protections owed to detainees within the United States may be different than the protections owed to persons held at Guantanamo or elsewhere. This may have implications for the continued detention or prosecution of persons who are transferred to the United States. The transfer of detainees to the United States may also have immigration consequences. Notably, some detainees might qualify for asylum or other protections under immigration law.

This report provides an overview of major legal issues likely to arise as a result of executive and legislative action to close the Guantanamo detention facility. It discusses legal issues related to the transfer or release of Guantanamo detainees (either to a foreign country or into the United States), the continued detention of such persons in the United States, and the possible removal of persons brought to the United States. The report also discusses selected constitutional issues that may arise in the criminal prosecution of detainees, emphasizing the procedural and substantive protections that are utilized in different adjudicatory forums (i.e., federal civilian courts, court-martial proceedings, and military commissions). Issues discussed include detainees' right to a speedy trial, the prohibition against prosecution under ex post facto laws, and limitations upon the admissibility of hearsay and secret evidence in criminal cases.

Chapter 2 - After the U.S. Supreme Court held that U.S. courts have jurisdiction pursuant to 28 U.S.C. § 2241 to hear legal challenges on behalf of persons detained at the U.S. Naval Station in Guantanamo Bay, Cuba, in connection with the war against terrorism (*Rasul v. Bush*), the Pentagon established administrative hearings, called "Combatant Status Review Tribunals" (CSRTs), to allow the detainees to contest their status as enemy combatants, and informed them of their right to pursue relief in federal court by seeking a writ of *habeas corpus*. Lawyers subsequently filed dozens of petitions on behalf of the detainees in the District Court for the District of Columbia, where district court judges reached inconsistentconclusions as to whether the detainees have any enforceable rights to challenge their treatment and detention.

In December 2005, Congress passed the Detainee Treatment Act of 2005 (DTA) to divest the courts of jurisdiction to hear some detainees' challenges by eliminating the federal courts' statutory jurisdiction over *habeas* claims by aliens detained at Guantanamo Bay (as well as other causes of action based on their treatment or living conditions). The DTA provides instead for limited appeals of CSRT determinations or final decisions of military commissions. After the Supreme Court rejected the view that the DTA left it without jurisdiction to review a *habeas* challenge to the validity of military commissions in the case of *Hamdan v. Rumsfeld*, the 109th Congress enacted the Military Commissions Act of 2006 (MCA) (P.L. 109-366) to authorize the President to convene military commissions and to amend the DTA to further reduce access to federal courts by "alien enemy combatants," wherever held, by eliminating pending and future causes of action other than the limited review of military proceedings permitted under the DTA.

In June 2008, the Supreme Court held in the case of *Boumediene v. Bush* that aliens designated as enemy combatants and detained at Guantanamo Bay have the constitutional privilege of *habeas corpus*. The Court also found that MCA § 7, which limited judicial review of executive determinations of the petitioners' enemy combatant status, did not provide an adequate *habeas* substitute and therefore acted asan unconstitutional suspension of the writ of *habeas*. The immediate impact of the *Boumediene* decision is that detainees at Guantanamo may petition a federal district court for *habeas* review of the legality and possibly the circumstances of their detention, perhaps including challenges to the jurisdiction of military commissions. Pertinent legislation includes H.R. 267, S. 185, S. 576, S. 1547, S. 1548, H.R. 1415, H.R. 1416, H.R. 1585, H.R. 4986, H.R. 1189, H.R. 2543, H.R. 2710, H.R. 2826, S. 1249, H.R. 5658, S. 3001, S. 3002, H.R. 2212 and H.R. 6274.

Chapter 3 - In the consolidated cases of *Boumediene v. Bush* and *Al Odah v. United States*, decided June 12, 2008, the Supreme Court held in a 5-4 opinion that aliens designated as enemy combatants and detained at the U.S. Naval Station in Guantanamo Bay, Cuba, have the constitutional privilege of *habeas corpus*. The Court also found that § 7 of the Military Commissions Act (MCA), which limited judicial review of executive determinations of the petitioners' enemy combatant status, did not provide an adequate *habeas* substitute and therefore acted as an unconstitutional suspension of the writ of *habeas*. The immediate impact of the *Boumediene* decision is that detainees at Guantanamo may petition a federal district court for *habeas* review of the circumstances of their detention. This report summarizes the *Boumediene* decision and analyzes several of its major implications for the U.S. detention of alien enemy combatants and legislation that limits detainees' access to judicial review. For discussion of litigation challenging detention policy, see CRS Report RL33180, *Enemy Combatant Detainees: Habeas Corpus Challenges in Federal Court*, by Jennifer K. Elsea, Michael John Garcia, and Kenneth R. Thomas.

In the consolidated cases of *Boumediene v. Bush* and *Al Odah v. United States*,[1] decided June 12, 2008, the Supreme Court held in a 5-4 opinion that aliens designated as enemy combatants and detained at the U.S. Naval Station in Guantanamo Bay, Cuba, have the constitutional privilege of *habeas corpus*. The Court also found that § 7 of the Military Commissions Act (MCA),[2] which limited judicial review of executive determinations of the petitioners' enemy combatant status, did not provide an adequate *habeas* substitute and therefore acted as an unconstitutional suspension of the writ of *habeas*. The immediate impact of the *Boumediene* decision is that detainees at Guantanamo may petition a federal district court for *habeas* review of the circumstances of their detention.

In: Closing Guantanamo - Issues and Legal... ISBN: 978-1-60741-511-4
Editor: Noah M. Claeys

Chapter 1

CLOSING THE GUANTANAMO DETENTION CENTER: LEGAL ISSUES*

Michael John Garcia, Elizabeth B. Bazan, R. Chuck Mason, Edward C. Liu, and Amma C. Henning

SUMMARY

Following the terrorist attacks of 9/11, Congress passed the Authorization to Use Military Force (AUMF), which granted the President the authority "to use all necessary and appropriate force against those ... [who] planned, authorized, committed, or aided the terrorist attacks" against the United States." As part of the subsequent "war on terror," many persons captured during military operations in Afghanistan and elsewhere were transferred to the U.S. Naval Station at Guantanamo Bay, Cuba for detention and possible prosecution before military tribunals. Although nearly 800 persons have been transferred to Guantanamo since early 2002, the substantial majority of Guantanamo detainees have ultimately been transferred to a third country for continued detention or release. The roughly 250 detainees who remain fall into three categories: (1) persons placed in non-penal, preventative detention to stop them from rejoining hostilities; (2) persons who have been brought, or are

* This is an edited, reformatted and augmented version of a CRS Report for Congress publication dated January 2009.

expected to be brought, before a military tribunal to face criminal charges for alleged war crimes; and (3) persons who have been cleared for transfer or release to a third country, whom the United States continues to detain pending transfer. Although the Supreme Court ruled in *Boumediene v. Bush* that Guantanamo detainees may seek *habeas corpus* review of the legality of their detention, several legal issues remain unsettled, including the scope of *habeas* review available to Guantanamo detainees, the remedy available for those persons found to be unlawfully held by the United States, and the extent to which other constitutional provisions extend to noncitizens held at Guantanamo.

On January 22, 2009, President Barack Obama issued an Executive Order requiring the Guantanamo detention facility to be closed as soon as practicable, and no later than a year from the date of the Order. Officials in the Obama Administration have stated that the Administration will work with Congress to craft legislation to effectuate the facility's closure and clarify the legal status of detainees transferred to the United States.

The closure of the Guantanamo detention facility may raise a number of legal issues with respect to the individuals formerly interned there, particularly if those detainees are transferred to the United States. The nature and scope of constitutional protections owed to detainees within the United States may be different than the protections owed to persons held at Guantanamo or elsewhere. This may have implications for the continued detention or prosecution of persons who are transferred to the United States. The transfer of detainees to the United States may also have immigration consequences. Notably, some detainees might qualify for asylum or other protections under immigration law.

This report provides an overview of major legal issues likely to arise as a result of executive and legislative action to close the Guantanamo detention facility. It discusses legal issues related to the transfer or release of Guantanamo detainees (either to a foreign country or into the United States), the continued detention of such persons in the United States, and the possible removal of persons brought to the United States. The report also discusses selected constitutional issues that may arise in the criminal prosecution of detainees, emphasizing the procedural and substantive protections that are utilized in different adjudicatory forums (i.e., federal civilian courts, court-martial proceedings, and military commissions). Issues discussed include detainees' right to a speedy trial, the prohibition against prosecution under ex post facto laws, and limitations upon the admissibility of hearsay and secret evidence in criminal cases.

INTRODUCTION

Following the terrorist attacks of 9/11, Congress passed the Authorization to Use Military Force (AUMF), which granted the President the authority "to use all necessary and appropriate force against those ... [who] planned, authorized, committed, or aided the terrorist attacks" against the United States.[1] As part of the subsequent "war on terror," many persons captured during military operations in Afghanistan and elsewhere were transferred to the U.S. Naval Station at Guantanamo Bay, Cuba for detention and possible prosecution before military tribunals.

Although nearly 800 persons have been transferred to Guantanamo since early 2002, the substantial majority of Guantanamo detainees have ultimately been transferred to a third country for continued detention or release.[2] The roughly 250 detainees who remain fall into three categories:

- Persons designated as enemy combatants who have been placed in preventative detention to stop them from returning to the battlefield. Preventative detention ofcaptured belligerents is non-penal in nature, and must be ended upon the cessation of hostilities.
- Persons designated as enemy combatants who, besides being subject to preventative detention, have been brought or are expected to be brought before a military tribunal to face criminal charges for alleged violations of the law of war.If convicted, such persons may be subject to criminal penalty, which in the caseof the most severe offenses may include life imprisonment or death.
- Persons who have been cleared for transfer or release to a foreign country, either because (1) they are not believed to have been enemy combatants or (2) although they were designated as enemy combatants, they are no longer considered a threat to U.S. security. Such persons remain detained at Guantanamo until their transfer may be effectuated.

The decision by the Bush Administration to detain suspected belligerents at Guantanamo was based upon both policy and legal considerations. From a policy standpoint, the U.S. facility at Guantanamo offered a safe and secure location away from the battlefield where captured persons could be interrogated and potentially tried by military tribunals for any war crimes they may have committed. From a legal standpoint, the Bush Administration sought to avoid the possibility that suspected enemy combatants could pursue legal challenges regarding their detention or other wartime actions taken by the Executive. The Bush Administration initially believed that Guantanamo was largely beyond the jurisdiction of the federal courts, and noncitizens held there would not have access to the same substantive and procedural protections that would be required if they were detained in the United States.[3]

The legal support for this policy was significantly eroded by a series of Supreme Court rulings permitting Guantanamo detainees to seek judicial review of the circumstances of their detention. Although Congress attempted to limit federal courts' **jurisdiction** over detainees through the enactment of the Detainee Treatment Act of 2005 (DTA, P.L. 109-148, Title X) and the Military Commissions Act of 2006 (MCA, P.L. 109-366), these efforts were subject to judicial challenge. In 2008, the Supreme Court ruled in *Boumediene v. Bush* that the constitutional writ of *habeas corpus* extends to noncitizens held at Guantanamo, and found that provisions of the DTA and MCA eliminating federal *habeas* jurisdiction over Guantanamo detainees acted as an unconstitutional suspension of the writ.[4] As a result, Guantanamo detainees may seek *habeas* review of the legality of their detention. Nonetheless, several legal issues remain unsettled, including the scope of *habeas* review available to Guantanamo detainees, the remedy available for those persons found to be unlawfully held by the United States, and the extent to which other constitutional provisions extend to noncitizens held at Guantanamo.[5]

On January 22, 2009, President Barack Obama issued an Executive Order requiring that the Guantanamo detention facility be closed as soon as practicable, and no later than a year from the date of the Order.[6] Any persons who continue to be held at Guantanamo at the time of closure are to be either transferred to a third country for continued detention or release, or transferred to another U.S. detention facility. The Order further requires specified officials to review all Guantanamo detentions to assess whether the detainee should continue to be held by the United States, transferred or released to a third country, or be prosecuted by the United States for criminal offenses.[7] Reviewing authorities are required to identify and consider the legal, logistical, and security issues that would arise in the event that some detainees are transferred to the United States. The Order also requires reviewing authorities to assess the feasibility of prosecuting detainees in an Article III court. During this review period, the Secretary of Defense is required to take steps to ensure that all proceedings before military commissions and the United States Court of Military Commission Review are halted.

The closure of the Guantanamo detention facility raises a number of legal issues with respect to the individuals presently interned there, particularly if those detainees are transferred to the United States. The nature and scope of constitutional protections owed to detainees within the United States may be different than those available to persons held at Guantanamo or elsewhere. This may have implications for the continued detention or prosecution of persons transferred to the United States. The transfer of detainees to the United States may have additional consequences, as some detainees might qualify for asylum or other protections under immigration law. Secretary of Defense Robert Gates has stated that the Administration will work with Congress to craft legislation effectuating this closure of the Guantanamo detention facility and addressing some of the legal issues that would arise if detainees were transferred to the United States.[8] The Executive Order issued by President Obama also contemplates that the Administration "work with Congress on any legislation that may be appropriate" relating to the transfer of detainees to the United States.[9]

It is possible that legislative proposals may be introduced to effectuate or limit the transfer, detention, and/or prosecution of Guantanamo detainees. For example, proposals may be introduced to modify executive authority to detain certain persons in wartime. Proposals may also be made to clarify the immigration status of detainees transferred into the United States. Legislation may also be considered requiring criminal prosecutions of detainees to occur in a specified forum (i.e., in federal civilian court, in courts-martial proceedings, or before military commissions), or amending procedural rules governing the prosecution of detainees. Proposals may also be considered to create an entirely new forum for the prosecution of detainees, such as a national security court. The scope and effect of such proposals may be shaped by constitutional constraints.

This report provides an overview of major legal issues that are likely to arise as a result of executive and legislative action to close the Guantanamo detention facility. It discusses legal issues related to the transfer or release of Guantanamo detainees (either to a foreign country or into the United States), the continued detention of such persons in the United States, and the possible removal of persons brought to the United States. It considers selected constitutional issues that may arise in the criminal prosecution of detainees, emphasizing the procedural and substantive protections that exist in different adjudicatory forums. Issues discussed include detainees' right to a speedy trial, the prohibition against prosecution under ex post facto laws, and limitations upon the admissibility of hearsay and secret evidence in criminal cases. These issues are likely to be relevant not only to the treatment of Guantanamo detainees, but also to other terrorist suspects and/or enemy combatants apprehended by the United States in the future.

Detainee Transfer or Release from Guantanamo

Any proposal to close the Guantanamo detention facility must necessarily address the transfer of persons currently detained there. While some detainees may be transferred to third countries for continued detention or release, proposals to close the Guantanamo detention facility have contemplated transferring at least some detainees to the United States.[10]

Transfer/Release of Guantanamo Detainees to a Third Country

The vast majority of persons initially transferred to Guantanamo for preventative detention have been transferred to third countries, either for continued detention by the receiving country or for release.[11] Decisions to transfer a detainee to a third country have been based upon a determination by U.S. officials that (1) the detainee is not an enemy combatant or (2) while the detainee was properly designated as an enemy combatant, his continued detention by the United States is no longer warranted.[12] A decision by military authorities that the continued detention of an enemy combatant is no longer appropriate is based on a number of factors, including a determination that the detainee no longer poses a threat to the U.S. and its allies. Generally, if continued detention is no longer deemed necessary, the detainee is transferred to the control of another government for his release.[13] The DoD also transfers enemy combatants to other countries for continued detention, investigation, and/or prosecution when those governments are willing to accept responsibility for ensuring that the transferred person will not pose a continuing threat to the United States and its allies.[14]

Domestic and international legal requirements may constrain the ability of the United States to transfer persons to foreign countries if they might face torture or other forms of persecution. Most notably, Article 3 of the U.N. Convention against Torture and Other Cruel, Inhuman, or Degrading Treatment or Punishment (CAT) and its implementing legislation prohibit the transfer of persons to countries where there are substantial grounds for believing (i.e., it would be "more likely than not") that they would be subjected to torture.[15] The Bush Administration took the position that CAT Article 3 and its implementing legislation did not cover the transfer of foreign persons held outside the United States in the "war on terror."[16]

Nonetheless, the DoD has stated that "it is the policy of the United States, consistent with the approach taken by the United States in implementing ... [CAT], not to repatriate or transfer ...[Guantanamo detainees] to other countries where it believes it is more likely than not that they will be tortured."[17] When the transfer of a Guantanamo detainee is deemed appropriate, the United States seeks diplomatic assurances that the person will be treated humanely by the foreign government accepting the transfer. If such assurances are not deemed sufficiently reliable, the transfer will not be executed until the concerns of U.S. officials are satisfactorily resolved.[18] The use of diplomatic assurances in Guantanamo transfer decisions is similar to the practice sometimes employed by U.S. authorities when determining whether the extradition of a person or the removal of an alien by immigration authorities would comply with CAT requirements.

Roughly 60 of the approximately 250 persons held at Guantanamo have been cleared for transfer or release, but remain at Guantanamo either because no country will accept the detainee, or because human rights concerns have caused the United States to refrain from transferring the detainee to a country willing to accept him. A significant number of detainees could also potentially be transferred to other countries for continued detention if the United States was assured that the receiving country could manage the threat they pose.[19] Whether future diplomatic efforts will effectuate the transfer of some or all of these persons to third countries remains to be seen.

In recent years, legislative proposals have been introduced that would impose more stringent requirements upon the transfer of military detainees to foreign countries, particularly when the transfer might raise human rights concerns. These proposals have generally sought to establish standards for the acceptance of diplomatic assurances by transfer authorities, and require subsequent monitoring of the treatment of a transferred detainee.[20] Similar proposals may be introduced in the 111th Congress. If enacted, such measures might impede the transfer of some Guantanamo detainees to third countries.

Transfer of Detainees into the United States

Most proposals to end the detention of foreign belligerents at Guantanamo contemplate the transfer of at least some detainees into the United States, either for continued preventative detention or prosecution before a military or civilian court. Whether existing federal laws limit executive discretion to transfer captured noncitizens into the United States for continued detention arguably remains an open question. The Immigration and Nationality Act (INA) generally bars the entry of aliens involved in terrorism-related activity, as well as the admission of aliens whose entry would pose a threat to U.S. security or otherwise have serious adverse foreign policy consequences.[21] Under current law, it would appear that most persons currently detained at Guantanamo would generally be barred from admission into the United States on terrorism- and other security-related grounds under normal circumstances. Even if a detainee is not inadmissible on such grounds, he may still be inadmissible under other INA provisions.[22] However, it could be argued that the INA's restrictions upon the entry of certain categories of aliens are not intended to cover those persons transferred by the DoD into the United States for purposes of military detention. It also could be argued that the 2001 AUMF, which grants the President authority to use all "necessary and appropriate force" against those responsible for the 9/11 attacks, impliedly authorizes the President to detain captured belligerents in the United States, even though such persons would generally be barred from entry under the INA.[23] Legislation may be considered which addresses the application of federal immigration laws to the transfer of detainees to the United States, and clarifies the immigration status of detainees transferred into the country.[24]

Assuming that the INA's restrictions on alien admissibility are applicable to military detainees, the executive branch could still effectuate their transfer into the United States pursuant to its "parole" authority. In the immigration context, parole is a discretionary authority that may be exercised on a case-by-case basis to permit inadmissible aliens to physically enter the United States, including when the alien's entry or stay serves a "significant public benefit."[25] The entry of a paroled alien does not constitute admission into the United States for immigration purposes. Despite physical entry into the country, the alien is "still in theory of law at the boundary line and had gained no foothold in the United State[s]."[26] Indeed, even if the INA does not make parole a legal requisite for the transfer of aliens into the United States, the executive branch may nonetheless opt to use its parole authority with respect to transferred detainees in order to clarify their immigration status in case they are required to be released from U.S. custody. As discussed later, however, an alien's parole into the United States may result in the alien becoming eligible for asylum or other forms of immigration-related relief from removal.

DETENTION AND TREATMENT OF PERSONS TRANSFERRED TO THE UNITED STATES

Many of the rules and standards governing the detention and treatment of persons at Guantanamo would remain applicable to detainees transferred into the United States. However, non-citizens held in the United States may be entitled to more protections under the Constitution than those detained abroad.

Authority to Detain within the United States

Guantanamo detainees properly determined to be "enemy combatants" may be held in preventative detention by military authorities even if transferred to the United States. In the 2004 case of *Hamdi v. Rumsfeld*, a majority of the Supreme Court recognized that, as a necessary incident to the 2001 AUMF, the President is authorized to detain persons captured while fighting U.S. forces in Afghanistan for the duration of the conflict.[27] A divided Supreme Court also declared that "a state of war is not a blank check for the president," and ruled that persons deemed "enemy combatants" have the right to challenge their detention before a judge or other "neutral decision-maker."[28]

While the preventative detention of "enemy combatants" is constitutionally acceptable, the scope of persons potentially falling under this category remains uncertain. The *Hamdi* plurality was limited to an understanding that the phrase "enemy combatant" includes an "individual who ... was part of or supporting forces hostile to the United States or coalition partners in Afghanistan and who engaged in an armed conflict against the United States there."[29] Left unresolved is the extent to which the 2001 AUMF permits the detention of persons captured away from the zone of combat, or whether the President has the independent authority to detain such persons in the exercise of his Commander-in-Chief power. The Court also did not define what constitutes "support" for hostile forces necessary to acquire "enemy combatant" status or activities which constitute "engage[ment] in an armed conflict." In December 2008, the Supreme Court agreed to hear an appeal of an *en banc* ruling by the Fourth Circuit in the case of *al-Marri v. Pucciarelli*, in which a majority of the Court of Appeals found that the 2001 AUMF permits the detention as an "enemy combatant" of a resident alien alleged to have planned to engage in hostile activities within the United States on behalf of Al Qaeda, but who had not been part of the conflict in Afghanistan.[30] The

Supreme Court's decision may have implications for the continued detention of persons in U.S. military custody who were captured away from the battlefield, including alleged members or associates of Al Qaeda or the Taliban who did not directly engage in hostilities against the United States or its coalition partners.

In the absence of legal authority to detain a person as an "enemy combatant," U.S. military authorities must generally release the person from custody. However, there may be grounds for the person's continued detention by U.S. law enforcement or immigration authorities. If a former detainee brought to the U.S. is charged with a federal crime, a judicial officer may order his pretrial detention following a hearing in which it is determined that no other conditions would reasonably assure the individual's appearance for trial or the safety of the community or another individual.[31] A former detainee may also potentially be held in detention as a material witness to a criminal proceeding, including a grand jury proceeding, if a judicial officer orders his arrest and detention after determining that it may become impracticable to secure the presence of the person by subpoena.[32]

If the military lacks authority to hold a detainee brought to the United States and is unable to effectuate his transfer to another country, the detainee might nonetheless be placed in immigration removal proceedings and continue being detained pending removal. Detention pending removal is generally required for aliens inadmissible on criminal or terrorism-related grounds.[33] Following a final order of removal,[34] an alien is typically required to be removed within 90 days. During this period, an alien is usually required to be detained, and in no circumstance may an alien inadmissible or deportable on any terrorism-related ground or most crime-related grounds be released from detention.[35] If the alien is unable to be removed during the 90-day period provided by statute, his continued detention for a period beyond six months may be statutorily and constitutionally prohibited.[36] However, those aliens who are specially dangerous to the community may be subject to continued detention, subject to periodic review. Immigration regulations permit the continued detention of certain categories of aliens due to special circumstances, including, *inter alia*, any alien who is detained on account of (1) serious adverse foreign policy consequences of release; (2) security or terrorism concerns; or (3) being considered specially dangerous due to having committed one or more crimes of violence and having a mental condition making it likely that the alien will commit acts of violence in the future.[37]

Proposals have been made to clarify executive authority to detain certain wartime detainees. These include proposals to provide express statutory authority for the Executive to detain persons who have engaged in hostilities or purposefully supported Al Qaeda, the Taliban, or associated organizations.[38] Proposals have also been made to require any alien detainee released from military custody into the United States to be taken into custody by immigration authorities pending removal. While the United States has interned "enemy aliens" who had not participated in hostilities against the United States in prior conflicts,[39] the scope and effect of proposals requiring the detention of specified categories of persons other than enemy combatants may potentially be subject to constitutional challenges.

Treatment of Detained Persons

The rules governing the treatment of Guantanamo detainees would largely remain unchanged if detainees were transferred to the United States. The DTA provides that no person in the custody or effective control of the DoD or detained in a DoD facility shall be subject to any interrogation treatment or technique that is not authorized by and listed in the United States Army Field Manual on Intelligence Interrogation, unless the person is being held pursuant to U.S. criminal or immigration laws (in which case the detainee's interrogation would be governed by applicable criminal or immigration law enforcement standards).[40] The Field Manual requires all detainees to be treated in a manner consistent with the Geneva Conventions, and prohibits the use of torture or cruel, inhuman, and degrading treatment in any circumstance. In the 2006 case of *Hamdan v. Rumsfeld*, the Supreme Court found that, at a minimum, Common Article 3 of the Geneva Conventions applied to persons captured in the conflict with Al Qaeda.[41] Common Article 3 requires persons to be treated humanely and protected from "violence to life and person," "cruel treatment and torture," and "outrages upon personal dignity, in particular, humiliating and degrading treatment." All of these requirements would remain applicable to detainees transferred into the United States, at least so long as they remained in military custody.

Noncitizen detainees transferred to the United States may also receive greater constitutional protections than those detained outside the United States. "It is well established that certain constitutional protections available to persons inside the United States are unavailable to aliens outside of our geographic borders."[42] Although the Supreme Court in *Boumediene* held that the constitutional writ of *habeas corpus* extends to Guantanamo, it did not elaborate as to the extent to which other constitutional provisions apply to noncitizens held at Guantanamo.[43] However, the DTA and MCA prohibit any person in U.S. custody or control (including those located at Guantanamo or elsewhere outside U.S. territory) from being subjected to cruel, inhuman, or degrading treatment of the kind prohibited by the Fifth, Eighth, and Fourteenth Amendments.[44]

Legal Challenges to Nature of Detention

If transferred to the United States, detainees may be able to seek judicial review over a broader range of actions taken against them. Besides eliminating detainees' access to *habeas corpus* review, the DTA and MCA stripped federal courts of jurisdiction to hear most claims by noncitizen detainees. Specifically, federal courts are denied jurisdiction over:

> any other action against the United States or its agents relating to any aspect of the detention, transfer, treatment, trial, or conditions of confinement of an alien who is or was detained by the United States and has been determined by the United States to have been properly detained as an enemy combatant or is awaiting such determination.[45]

Although the *Boumediene* Court held that the constitutional writ of *habeas* permitted Guantanamo detainees to challenge the legality of their detention, the Court declined to "discuss the reach of the writ with respect to claims of unlawful conditions of treatment or confinement."[46] Because the *Boumediene* Court left these questions unresolved, the viability of measures stripping courts of jurisdiction to hear claims regarding the conditions of detention may depend upon a reviewing court's interpretation of the constitutional protections owed to detainees. While measures that eliminate detainees' ability to pursue statute- or treaty-based challenges to aspects of their detention may be deemed permissible by a reviewing court, measures that seek to eliminate (rather than merely circumscribe) detainees' ability to bring constitutional challenges regarding the circumstances of their detention would likely be subject to serious legal challenge. Although the scope of constitutional protections owed to Guantanamo detainees remains a matter of legal dispute, it is clear that the procedural and substantive due process protections of the Constitution apply to all persons within the United States, regardless of their citizenship.[47] Accordingly, detainees transferred to the United States might be able to more successfully pursue legal challenges against aspects of their detention that allegedly infringe upon constitutional protections owed to them.

REMOVAL OF DETAINEES FROM THE UNITED STATES

If there are no longer grounds to hold a detainee, the United States must terminate custody either through transfer or release. Persons held in the United States may have greater legal redress against their unwilling transfer to a third country than those held abroad, and may potentially seek judicial review of transfer decisions through *habeas* proceedings.

CAT Article 3 and its implementing legislation prohibit the transfer of detainees from the United States to countries where they would more likely than not face torture. This prohibition is absolute and without regard to whether an individual has been involved in terrorist or criminal activity. While the Bush Administration took the position that CAT Article 3 and its implementing legislation do not govern the transfer of detainees held outside the United States, there appears to be little if any dispute regarding CAT's application to transfers from the United States.[48]

Detainees transferred to the United States might seek relief from removal under U.S. immigration laws. An alien who is physically present or arrives in the United States, regardless of immigration status, may apply for asylum, a discretionary form of relief from removal available to aliens who have a well-founded fear of persecution if transferred to a third country. Persons granted asylum may thereafter apply for adjustment of status to that of a legal permanent resident. Certain potentially over-lapping categories of aliens are disqualified from asylum eligibility, including those involved in terrorism-related activity (including members of the Taliban and Al Qaeda) and those who are reasonably believed to pose a danger to U.S. security.[49] Nonetheless, it is possible that some detainees who have been found not to have fought on behalf of the Taliban or Al Qaeda may qualify for asylum or other forms of relief from removal if transferred to the United States. Further, if a detainee is declared ineligible for asylum or another form of relief from removal and is thereafter ordered removed by immigration officials, immigration authorities may be required to provide evidence forming the basis of this determination in the face of a legal challenge by the detainee.[50]

Proposals may be considered that would clarify the application of immigration laws to Guantanamo detainees transferred to the United States.

Secretary of Defense Gates has stated that the Obama Administration will seek legislation from Congress addressing detainees' immigration status, possibly including barring them from asylum eligibility.[51]

Detainees' Rights in a Criminal Prosecution

While many persons currently held at Guantanamo are only being detained as a preventative measure to stop them from returning to battle, the United States has brought or intends to pursue criminal charges against some detainees. Various constitutional provisions, most notably those arising from the Fifth and Sixth Amendments to the U.S. Constitution, apply to defendants throughout the process of criminal prosecutions. Prosecuting the Guantanamo detainees inside the United States would raise at least two major legal questions. First, does a detainee's status as an "enemy combatant" reduce the degree of constitutional protections to which he is entitled? Secondly, would the choice of judicial forum – i.e., civilian court, military commission, or courts-martial – affect interpretations of constitutional rights implicated in detainee prosecutions?

As previously discussed, the nature and extent to which the Constitution applies to noncitizens detained at Guantanamo is a matter of continuing legal dispute. Although the Supreme Court held in *Boumediene* that the constitutional writ of *habeas* extends to detainees held at Guantanamo, it left open the nature and degree to which other constitutional protections, including those relating to substantive and procedural due process, may also apply. The *Boumediene* Court noted that the Constitution's application to noncitizens in places like Guantanamo located outside the United States turns on "objective factors and practical concerns."[52] The Court has also repeatedly recognized that at least some constitutional protections are "unavailable to aliens outside our geographic borders."[53] The application of constitutional principles to the prosecution of aliens located at Guantanamo remains unsettled.

On the other hand, it is clear that if Guantanamo detainees are subject to criminal prosecution in United States, the constitutional provisions related to such proceedings would apply.[54] However, the application of these constitutional requirements might differ depending upon the forum in which charges are brought. The Fifth Amendment's requirement that no person be held to answer for a capital or infamous crime unless on a presentment or indictment of a grand jury, and the Sixth Amendment's requirements concerning trial by jury, have been found to be inapplicable to trials by military commissions or courts-martial.[55] The application of due process protections in military court proceedings may also differ from civilian court proceedings, in part because the Constitution "contemplates that Congress has 'plenary control over rights, duties, and responsibilities in the framework of the Military Establishment, including regulations, procedures, and remedies related to military discipline.'"[56] In the past, courts have been more accepting of security measures taken against "enemy aliens" than U.S. citizens, particularly as they relate to authority to detain or restrict movement on grounds of wartime security.[57] It is possible that the rights owed to enemy combatants in criminal prosecutions would be interpreted more narrowly by a reviewing court than those owed to defendants in other, more routine cases, particularly when the constitutional right at issue is subject to a balancing test.

There are several forums in which detainees could potentially be prosecuted for alleged criminal activity, including in federal civilian court, in general courts-martial proceedings, or before military commissions. The procedural protections afforded to the accused in each of these forums may differ, along with the types of offenses for which the accused may be prosecuted. The MCA authorized the establishment of military commissions with jurisdiction to try alien "unlawful enemy combatants" for offenses made punishable by the MCA or the law of war, and affords the accused fewer procedural protections than would be available to defendants in military courts-martial or federal civilian court proceedings.[58] Approximately 20 detainees at Guantanamo are currently facing charges before such commissions, though critics have raised questions regarding the constitutionality of the system established by the MCA.[59] The MCA does not restrict military commissions from exercising jurisdiction within the United States, and the Supreme Court has previously upheld the use of military commissions against enemy belligerents tried in the United States.[60] Although they have yet to be used for this purpose, detainees could also be brought before military courts-martial, which have jurisdiction over persons subject to military tribunal jurisdiction under the law of war via the Uniform Code of Military Justice (UCMJ).[61] Detainees brought before military-courts martial could be charged with offenses under the UCMJ and the law of war, though courts-martial rules concerning the accused's right to a speedy trial may pose an obstacle to prosecution absent modification.[62] Detainees could also potentially be prosecuted in federal civilian court for offenses under federal criminal statutes. Provisions in the U.S. Criminal Code relating to war crimes and terrorist activity apply extraterritorially and may be applicable to some detainees, though ex post facto and statute of limitation concerns may limit their application to certain offenses.[63]

Presently, the Executive has discretion in deciding the appropriate forum in which to prosecute detainees. As previously discussed, President Obama has issued an Executive Order that (at least temporarily) halts military commission proceedings, and also requires designated officials to assess the feasibility of prosecuting some detainees in federal civilian court. It is possible that legislative proposals may be introduced which require that prosecution occur in a particular forum or modify the procedural rules applicable to the prosecution of detainees. Proposals may also be considered to create an entirely new forum for the prosecution of detainees, such as a national security court.[64] The scope and effect of such proposals may be shaped by constitutional constraints, including with respect to the rights owed to the accused in criminal proceedings.

The following sections discuss selected constitutional issues that may arise in the criminal prosecution of detainees, emphasizing the procedural and substantive protections that are utilized in different adjudicatory forums.

Right to Assistance of Counsel

Detainees brought to the United States would have a constitutional right to assistance of counsel in any criminal prosecution. The procedural rules for federal civilian courts, courts-martial, and military commissions under the MCA all provide a defendant with the right to assistance of counsel. Depending upon the forum in which the detainee is tried, the particular procedural rules concerning a defendant's exercise of this right may differ.

The Sixth Amendment guarantees a criminal defendant the right "to have the Assistance of Counsel for his defence." This constitutional protection affords a defendant the right to retain counsel of his or her choosing and an opportunity to consult with that counsel.[65] Where a criminal defendant cannot afford to retain a lawyer to assist in his or her defense, such counsel will be appointed by the court.[66] The court must advise a criminal defendant of his or her right to counsel and must ask the defendant whether he or she wishes to waive that right.[67] A defendant can waive a right to assistance of counsel only if that waiver is knowing, voluntary, and intelligent.[68] However, the defendant need not fully and completely comprehend all of the consequences of that waiver.[69] This right also encompasses the right of a defendant to represent himself or herself, if the defendant intelligently and knowingly chooses to do so.[70] The Sixth Amendment right to counsel is the right to the effective assistance of counsel.[71] The standard for determining whether a defendant has received ineffective assistance of counsel is two-fold. The attorney's performance must have been deficient, and the prejudice to the defense resulting from the attorney's deficient performance must be so serious as to bring into question the outcome of the proceeding.[72] If there is an actual breakdown in the adversarial process, such as a case involving "circumstances that are so likely to prejudice the accused that the cost of litigating their effect in a particular case is unjustified," the Sixth Amendment is violated.[73]

In the federal civilian courts, the right to counsel is implemented under Rule 44 of the Federal Rules of Criminal Procedure. In part, this rule affords a criminal defendant who is unable to obtain counsel the right to have counsel appointed to represent him at every stage of the proceedings from initial appearance through appeal, unless the defendant waives this right.[74] In courts-martial, the right to counsel is implemented under Rule 506 of the Rules for Courts-Martial (R.C.M.). Rule 506 provides that a defendant has the right to be represented at a general or special court-martial by civilian counsel, if provided at no expense to the Government, and either by military counsel detailed under Article 27 of the UCMJ[75] or military counsel of the defendant's own selection. As in a civilian court, the defendant may also waive the right to be represented by counsel and may conduct the defense personally.[76]

A detainee subject to a military commission has the right to represented by counsel. The right is implemented by Rule 506 of the Rules for Military Commissions (R.M.C.). Rule 506 provides a detainee with a detailed defense counsel. The detainee also has the right to be represented by civilian counsel, if retained at no cost to the Government. Civilian counsel must fulfill certain qualifications, including being a U.S. citizen and having security clearance of Secret or higher.[77] Much like under the Rules for Courts-Martial, a defendant in a military commission proceeding may waive his right to counsel and may conduct the defense personally.[78] However, in a departure from the rules governing courts-martial, the detainee does not have the right to be granted specific individual military counsel upon request.

Right against Use of Coerced Confessions

One issue that could arise in the prosecution of certain detainees involves the admissibility of statements obtained during interrogation by U.S. or foreign military and intelligence agencies. Some detainees currently held at

Guantanamo were subjected to interrogation techniques that, if performed in the United States, would almost certainly be deemed unconstitutionally harsh.[79] The use of any such evidence in the criminal trial of a detainee would likely be subject to legal challenge under the Fifth Amendment on the ground that the statement was gained through undue coercion. As a general rule, statements made in response to coercive interrogation methods are inadmissible in U.S. courts. Fifth Amendment protections concerning the right against self-incrimination and due process serve as dual bases for exclusion of such evidence.[80]

Under the leading Supreme Court case, *Miranda v. Arizona*, courts will not admit defendants' statements at trial unless law enforcement officers issued the well-known *Miranda* warnings, which typically begin with "You have the right to remain silent," before the statements were made.[81] As a general rule, *Miranda* applies any time police question a defendant who is in "custody," broadly defined.[82] In the context of terrorist suspects' statements, at least one court has held that *Miranda* applies in Article III courts even if the questioning took place outside of the United States.[83]

However, the Court's recent jurisprudence has weakened *Miranda*'s effect by making clear that despite the holding's constitutional status,[84] there are cases in which it is appropriate to depart from strict adherence to *Miranda* warnings.[85] The *Miranda* exception possibly relevant to the Guantanamo detainees is the "public safety" exception, which the Court introduced in *New York v. Quarles*.[86] In *Quarles*, police officers inquired "Where is the gun?" to a suspect who had fled into a supermarket after a shooting.[87] The Court held that the suspect's incriminating response, "The gun is over there," was admissible in court, despite a lack of *Miranda* warnings, because the question had been necessary to secure the public's safety in that moment.[88] Despite the Court's emphasis in *Quarles* on the time-sensitive nature of the safety risk in that case,[89] some commentators have argued that the *Quarles* "public safety" exception should be extended to reach interrogations of captured terrorist suspects.[90]

A second *Miranda* exception possibly applicable to some detainees is an exception for statements made in response to questioning by foreign officials. In *United States v. Yosef*, the U.S. Court of Appeals for the Second Circuit held that "statements taken by foreign police in the absence of Miranda warnings are admissible if voluntary."[91] The *Yosef* court identified two situations in which this exception does not apply: (1) situations where U.S. interrogators are working with foreign interrogators as part of a "joint venture"; and (2) situations that "shock the judicial conscience."[92]

If the *Quarles* public safety exception, the foreign-interrogator exception, or another *Miranda* exception applied to statements made during questioning of a Guantanamo detainee, prosecutors would need to show only that the detainees' statements were made "voluntarily" before a court would admit them at trial.[93] For example, in *United States v. Abu Ali*, a case involving a defendant who had been arrested and questioned by the Saudi government for allegedly assisting terrorists in an attack, the U.S. Court of Appeals for the Fourth Circuit upheld statements made to the Saudi interrogators, despite a lack of *Miranda* warnings, because the court found that the statements were voluntary.[94]

The constitutional standard of "voluntariness" is recognized as "the ultimate safeguard against coerced confessions."[95] The definition for "voluntary" in this context matches the definition employed in other due-process cases; specifically, the test for voluntariness is "whether the confession was 'extracted by any sort of threats or violence, [or] obtained by any direct or implied promises, however slight, [or] by the exertion of any improper influence.'"[96] The voluntariness test is a totality-of-the-circumstances inquiry, in which courts examine factors such as "the youth of the accused, his lack of education, or his low intelligence, the lack of any advice to the accused of his constitutional rights, the length of detention, the repeated and prolonged nature of the questioning, and the use of physical punishment such as the deprivation of food or sleep."[97] The failure to provide *Miranda* warnings can serve as one factor in the totality-ofcircumstances evaluation.[98]

Under Article 31 of the UCMJ, individuals "subject to the code" who are brought before a court-martial are protected from the use of statements obtained through the use of coercion, unlawful influence, or unlawful inducement.[99] Additionally, an individual may not be forced to incriminate himself or to answer a question before any military tribunal that is not material to the issue and may tend to degrade him.[100] A suspect is also generally entitled to *Miranda* type warnings, commonly referred to as *31 bravo* rights, which require that a suspect be informed of the nature of the accusation against him; be advised that he does not have to make a statement regarding the offense; and be informed that any statement may be used as evidence in a trial by court-martial. The protections of Article 31 are broader than *Miranda* warnings in that a suspect must receive the warnings even if he is not in custody.[101] While a strict reading of the UCMJ might support the proposition that a captured insurgent suspected of engaging in unlawful hostilities could not be questioned by military personnel about such activities without first receiving a warning and possibly the opportunity to consult an attorney, developments in military case law cast that conclusion in doubt.[102] A review of Army regulations pertaining to the treatment of war-time captives suggests that military authorities do not regard Article 31 as applicable to captured belligerents suspected of violating the law of war, regardless of their prisoner-of-war status.[103] Military courts have also recognized a "public safety" exception to *Miranda* requirements similar to the rule applied in federal courts.[104]

Persons subject to a military commission also have a statutory privilege against self-incrimination, though this standard is less robust than that applicable in courts-martial proceedings.[105] Statements obtained by the use of torture are also statutorily prohibited.[106] However, the MCA authorized military commissions to permit the admission of statements obtained in the course of harsh interrogation not rising to the level of torture, if certain criteria are met. Statements made obtained on or after December 30, 2005 may not be admitted if the interrogation methods used to obtain them amounted to "cruel, inhuman, or degrading treatment" prohibited by the DTA.[107] This prohibition applies to statements obtained through methods that, if they had occurred within the United States, would be considered unconstitutionally harsh.[108] This requirement does not apply with respect to the admission of statements made prior to December 30, 2005.[109] In either case, if the degree of coercion used to obtain the statement is disputed, the military judge may only permit its admission if the totality of circumstances renders that statement reliable and the interests of justice are served by its admission.[110]

The standards for admission of evidence in military commissions may be subject to legal challenge, particularly by those defendants who seek to bar the admission of statements as involuntary, when the incriminating statements were made prior to the enactment of the DTA and were purportedly obtained through cruel, inhuman, or degrading treatment. Issues may also arise regarding the admissibility of any incriminating statements made after a detainee has been subjected to harsh interrogation. In November 2008, a military commission judge ruled that statements made by a detainee to U.S. authorities were tainted by his earlier confession to Afghan police hours before, which had purportedly been made under threat of death.[111] The judge concluded that the coercive effects of the death threats producing the detainee's first confession had not dissipated by the time of the second.

Right against Prosecution Under *Ex Post Facto* Laws

The ability to seek penal sanction against some detainees may be limited by ex post facto rules. Art. I, § 9, cl. 3, of the U.S. Constitution provides, "No Bill of Attainder or ex post facto Law shall be passed." The Ex Post Facto Clause[112] "protects liberty by preventing the government from enacting statutes with 'manifestly unjust and oppressive' retroactive effects."[113] This limitation may impede the ability of U.S. authorities to pursue criminal charges against some detainees, or alternatively inform decisions as to whether to pursue criminal charges in a military or civilian court, as offenses punishable under the jurisdiction of one forum may not be cognizable under the laws of another. While laws having retroactive effect may potentially be challenged on due process grounds,[114] the Ex Post Facto Clause acts as an independent limitation on congressional power, going "to the very root of Congress's ability to act at all, irrespective of time or place."[115] Accordingly, the Ex Post Facto Clause may be pertinent to the prosecution of detainees regardless of whether they are brought to the United States or held for trial at Guantanamo.

It appears that some detainees could be prosecuted for activities in federal civilian court without running afoul of the Ex Post Facto Clause, including for offenses related to or preceding the 9/11 terrorist attacks. While the number of laws criminalizing terrorism-related activity expanded in the aftermath of the 9/11 terrorist attacks, some criminal statutes concerning terrorist activity and having extraterritorial application were in effect in the years preceding, including laws relating to acts of terrorism within the United States that transcend national boundaries; killing or causing serious bodily injury to an American overseas for terrorist purposes; and money laundering in support of certain terrorism-related activity.[116] Some persons could also be charged with offenses under the War Crimes Act, which imposes criminal penalties for specified offenses under the law of war, including "grave breaches" of the Geneva Conventions.[117] It should be noted, however, that statute of limitations concerns may affect the ability of U.S. authorities to prosecute persons for some of these offenses. The statute of limitations for most federal offenses is five years, though the period for terrorism-related offenses is typically eight years, and there is no statute of limitations for capital offenses.[118]

The constitutional prohibition against ex post facto laws may also have implications in courts-martial or military commission proceedings, limiting the offenses with which detainees may be charged.[119] The UCMJ provides that general courts-martial have jurisdiction to "try any person who by the law of war is subject to trial by a military tribunal and may adjudge any punishment permitted by the law of war."[120] The UCMJ does not enumerate the offenses punishable under the law of war, instead relying on the common law of war to define the subject-matter jurisdiction in general courts-martial. In *Hamdan v. Rumsfeld*, a plurality of the Supreme Court recognized that for an act to be triable under the common law of war the precedent for it being treated as an offense must be "plain and unambiguous."[121] After examining the history of military commission practice in the United States and internationally, the plurality further concluded that conspiracy to violate the law of war was not in itself a crime under the common law of war or the UCMJ.[122]

Following the *Hamdan* ruling, Congress enacted the MCA, which authorized the establishment of military commissions to try certain detainees and exempted the commissions from many UCMJ requirements applicable to courts-martial proceedings. While military commissions differ from the general courts-martial system in that their personal jurisdiction is limited to "unlawful enemy combatants" (in contrast to the jurisdiction of general courts-martial, which may extend to "lawful" and "unlawful" combatants[123]), military commissions share subject-matter jurisdiction with the general courts-martial system over violations of the law of war. However, the systems differ in that Congress also lists several specific offenses punishable by military commissions, including, *inter alia*, murder of protected persons; murder in violation of the law of war; attacking civilians, civilian objects, or protected property; denying quarter; terrorism; providing material support for terrorism; and conspiracy to commit an offense punishable by military commission.[124] The MCA provides that such acts are punishable by military commissions regardless of whether they were "committed by an alien unlawful enemy combatant before, on, or after September 11, 2001."[125] In enacting the MCA, Congress asserted that it did "not establish new crimes that did not exist before its enactment," but rather codified "offenses that have traditionally been triable by military commissions."[126]

While many of the offenses listed in the MCA can be considered well-established offenses against the law of war, a court might conclude that some of the listed crimes are new, and that a detainee could not be prosecuted for such an offense on account of prior conduct. As previously mentioned, a plurality of the *Hamdan* Court found that conspiracy to commit a violation of the law of war is not itself a war crime.[127] The crime of "murder in violation of the law of war," which punishes persons who, as unprivileged belligerents, commit hostile acts that result in the death of any persons, including lawful combatants, in the context of an armed conflict, may also be new.[128] Similarly, there appears to be no precedent for defining "material support for terrorism" as a war crime, though such conduct arguably could be analogized to other types of conduct that have been punishable by military commissions in the past.[129]

Whether a reviewing court would deem some of the punishable offenses listed by the MCA as constitutionally impermissible, at least when applied to activities occurring prior to the MCA's enactment, may turn on the degree of deference given to Congress in defining violations of the law of war. The Constitution expressly grants Congress the power to "define and punish Offences ... against the Law of Nations."[130] While the Supreme Court has applied stringent criteria when determining whether an act is punishable under the law of war in the absence of a congressional declaration,[131] the standard may be more lenient when Congress acts pursuant to its constitutional authority to define war crime offenses.[132] Accordingly, it is possible that a reviewing court may defer to Congress's finding the specified offenses under the MCA are not new offenses, and find that prosecution of those offenses under military commissions (or possibly under the general courts-martial system, if the court relies on the MCA to inform its judgment of activities punishable under the common law of war) does not run afoul of the Ex Post Facto Clause. On the other hand, a reviewing court might find that any deference owed to congressional determinations is insufficient to permit the prosecution of some offenses to go forward.

Although federal courts have not yet had the opportunity to rule on ex post facto claims concerning military commissions, the issue has arisen at the commission level. During military commission proceedings in the case of *United States v. Hamdan*, the commission considered a defense motion to dismiss charges of conspiracy and providing material support for terrorism on the grounds that they violated the prohibition against ex post facto laws in the U.S. Constitution, Common Article 3 of the Geneva Conventions, and the law of nations. The Government opposed the motion on the grounds that the Constitution did not protect aliens held outside the United States, and that, even if the Constitution did apply, there was precedent for trial of these offenses by military commissions as violations of the Law of Armed Conflict.[133]

After determining that the Ex Post Facto Clause extends to congressional statutes applicable to Guantanamo, the commission turned to an examination of whether the MCA's prohibitions against conspiracy and material support for terrorism were ex post facto laws. The commission examined countervailing arguments as to whether these two offenses were violations of the law of war before enactment of the MCA and whether similar offenses had been tried by military commission in the past. After exploring conflicting evidence with respect to each of these crimes,[134] the commission deferred to the Congress' determination that these were not new offenses, finding that there was "adequate historical basis for this determination."[135] In so doing, the commission distinguished instances where the Congress has been silent from those where Congress has enacted legislation, stating:

> . . . Absent Congressional action under the define and punish clause to identify offenses as violations of the Law of War, the Supreme Court has looked for "clear and unequivocal" evidence that an offense violates the common law of war ... or that there is "universal agreement and practice" for the proposition. But where Congress has acted under its Constitutional authority to define and punish offenses against the law of nations, a greater level of deference to that determination is appropriate....[136]

The commission's ruling in *Hamdan* was not appealed to the federal courts, and therefore it is unclear whether a reviewing court would reach a similar conclusion regarding whether certain offenses under the MCA raised ex post facto concerns.

In addition to the constitutional question explored by the military commission in *Hamdan*, ex post facto concerns could potentially be raised in other situations. These considerations may inform decisions by U.S. authorities as to whether to pursue criminal charges against detainees in civilian court, under the general courts-martial system, or via the military commissions established by the MCA. They may also be relevant in the crafting of any new legislative proposals concerning the prosecution of detainees. If a statute increasing the penalty for an existing crime were to be given retroactive effect, it would raise ex post facto concerns. Additionally, in the event that a statute of limitations on a particular offense expired, a detainee would no longer face the possibility of prosecution for that offense. If that statute of limitations were then extended and that extension given retroactive effect, this would also be deemed an ex post facto law.[137] A further ex post facto issue could arise if the rules of evidence applicable at the time of prosecution for an offense set a lower evidentiary bar for conviction than those applicable at the time of the commission of the offense.[138]

Rules against Hearsay Evidence

Hearsay is a prior out-of-court statement of a person, offered at trial either orally by another person or in written form, in order to prove the truth of the matter asserted. In a trial before either a civilian or military court , the admissibility of hearsay may raise both evidentiary and constitutional issues. Civilian and military courts each have procedural rules limiting the admission of hearsay evidence. Further, the Sixth Amendment's Confrontation Clause states that the accused in any criminal prosecution retains the right to be "confronted with the witnesses against him."

As a practical matter, hearsay issues may arise in any prosecution of persons captured in the "war on terror" for reasons peculiar to that context. For example, witnesses detained by foreign governments may be unavailable to come to the United States to testify in a federal court,[139] or the government may be unwilling to make military and intelligence assets and personnel available for testimony.[140] Procedural rules and constitutional requirements may limit the use of hearsay evidence in the prosecution of some detainees.

Evidentiary Issues

Federal civilian courts, courts-martial, and military commissions all possess procedural rules governing the admission of hearsay evidence. Procedural rules applicable to federal courts under the Federal Rules of Evidence (FED. R. EVID.) and courts-martial proceedings under the Military Rules of Evidence (MIL. R. EVID.) impose largely similar restrictions on the usage of hearsay evidence. Under the FED. R. EVID. and the MIL. R. EVID., hearsay is generally inadmissible unless it qualifies under an exception to the hearsay rule.[141] For the most part, these exceptions require the hearsay evidence to be of a particular nature or context that gives them a greater degree of reliability than other out-of court statements. Examples of exceptions to the hearsay rule include "excited utterances" made in relation to a startling event, which were made while the declarant was under the stress of excitement caused by the event; records of regularly-conducted activity; and statements of a self-incriminating nature.[142] The FED. R. EVID. and the MIL. R. EVID. also recognize a residual exception for statements which have "equivalent circumstantial guarantees of trustworthiness."[143] Examples of statements that have been held to qualify under the residual exception include interviews of child abuse victims by specially trained FBI agents[144] and statements contained within the files of a foreign intelligence agency.[145]

One important aspect of the definition of hearsay is that statements made by co-conspirators in furtherance of a conspiracy are not considered hearsay.[146] For example, in prosecutions alleging material support to terrorist organizations, evidence of statements by co-conspirators may be introduced against a defendant at trial even if those statements would not have qualified under a hearsay exception. Before these statements may be admitted, it is necessary to establish that the conspiracy exists. The co-conspirators statements being offered may be considered when making this initial determination, but are not sufficient standing alone to establish the existence of a conspiracy.[147]

In comparison with the FED. R. EVID. or the MIL. R. EVID., the procedural rules for military commissions under the Military Commission Rules of Evidence (MIL. COMM. R. EVID.) are much more permissive regarding the admissibility of hearsay evidence. Hearsay evidence may be admitted if either (1) it would be admitted under rules of evidence applicable in trial by general courts-martial; or (2) more broadly, if the proponent of the evidence makes known to the adverse party the intention to offer such evidence, and as well as the particulars of the evidence.[148] In the latter case, the accused may only have such evidence excluded if he can demonstrate by a preponderance of evidence that the hearsay evidence is unreliable under the totality of the circumstances.[149]

As a result of the less stringent rules regarding the admissibility of hearsay in Military Commissions, prosecutors may have a broader range of inculpatory evidence at their disposal.

Hearsay evidence that is inadmissible under the FED. R. EVID. or MIL. R. EVID. might be admitted under the MIL. COMM. R. EVID. because the defendant is unable to meet the burden of showing the statements are unreliable. In contrast, under the FED. R. EVID. or the MIL. R. EVID., it is the *proponent's* burden to show that a statement has sufficient indicia of reliability to qualify for the residual exception. On the other hand, the MIL. COMM. R. EVID. permits a broader scope of hearsay for both parties. In some cases, a defendant may be able to introduce more *exculpatory* evidence under the MIL. COMM. R. EVID. than in a federal court or court martial. Because prosecutors generally choose the forum in which to prosecute a case, U.S. authorities may have the option of choosing among the different hearsay rules to their advantage, depending upon the particular facts of a case.

Constitutional Issues

The Constitution imposes its own limitations on the admission of hearsay evidence in criminal cases. The protections afforded under the Confrontation Clause apply to both civilian and military proceedings.[150] While courts have yet to rule as to whether the Confrontation Clause's protections against hearsay extend to noncitizens brought before military commissions held at Guantanamo,[151] it would certainly appear to restrict the use of hearsay evidence in cases brought against detainees transferred to the United States.

In *Crawford v. Washington,* the Supreme Court held that even where a hearsay exception may apply under applicable forum rules, the Confrontation Clause prohibits the admission of hearsay against a criminal defendant if the character of the statement is testimonial and the defendant has not had a prior opportunity for cross-examination.[152] Although the definition of testimonial statements has not been thoroughly explicated, lower courts have interpreted the proper inquiry to be "whether a reasonable person in the declarant's position would have expected his statements to be used at trial."[153] In the traditional law enforcement context, the Court has expressly held that statements taken by police officers in the course of either investigations of past criminal activity or formal interrogation would qualify as testimonial under any reasonable definition of the term.[154] In contrast, the Supreme Court has held that statements made "to enable police assistance to meet an ongoing emergency"[155] were not testimonial, because, objectively determined, the purpose of the statements was to request assistance and not to act "as a witness."[156]

Many of the individuals detained at the naval base at Guantanamo Bay were apprehended on the battlefield in Afghanistan or other locations, as a consequence of their alleged actions there. Evidence against these potential defendants may include statements regarding their activities by persons also engaged in that conflict and subsequently captured. Sixth Amendment concerns may be raised if prosecutory authorities attempt to introduce statements made by other persons or detainees without presenting those declarants to personally testify in court. In these situations, the admissibility of the statements against the defendants would appear to turn on whether the character of the statements made is testimonial or not.[157]

In light of the Supreme Court's rulings in the domestic law enforcement context, it seems reasonable to conclude that the statements of enemy combatant witnesses obtained during formal interrogation by law enforcement would be considered testimonial. Similarly, incriminating statements made to U.S. or foreign military personnel by enemy combatants on the battlefield might also be considered testimonial. Insofar as these statements are determined to be testimonial, the Sixth Amendment would not appear to permit their use against a defendant without an opportunity for the defendant to cross-examine the declarant.

This constitutional requirement is not affected by less stringent rules regarding the admission, or even the definition, of hearsay that may be used in different forums. While the reach of the Confrontation Clause to noncitizens held at Guantanamo has not been definitively resolved, that clause would clearly apply to military commissions held within the United States. Therefore, although the FED. R. EVID., MIL. R. EVID., and MIL. COMM. R. EVID. may permit different amounts of hearsay initially, prosecutors in each forum would be subject to the requirements of the Confrontation Clause regarding testimonial hearsay against the defendant, at least with respect to proceedings occurring within the United States. Lastly, non-testimonial hearsay against the defendant, including statements which a reasonable person would not expect to be used at trial, are unaffected by the *Crawford* decision, and even testimonial hearsay may be admitted if the defense has had a prior opportunity to cross-examine the declarant.

Right to a Speedy Trial

In early 2008, the DoD announced that approximately 80 detainees being held at Guantanamo were expected to face trial before military commissions.[158] The Sixth Amendment guarantees a right to a speedy trial for the accused in all criminal prosecutions.[159] The protection is triggered "when a criminal prosecution has begun."[160] The invocation of the right may occur prior to indictment or formal charge, when "the actual restraints imposed by arrest and holding" are made.[161] The right has been found to extend to civilian and military courts,[162] though the nature of the right's application to military courts may differ from its application in the civilian context.[163] Statutory requirements and forum rules may also impose speedy trial requirements on applicable proceedings. Detainees transferred to the United States may argue that they are constitutionally entitled to a speedy trial,[164] and that denial of this right compels a reviewing court to dismiss the charges against them.[165]

A reviewing court's assessment of any speedy trial claim raised by a detainee is likely to balance any prejudice suffered by the accused with the public's interest in delaying prosecution. Courts have employed a multi-factor balancing test to assess whether a defendant's right to a speedy trial has been violated, taking into account the length of the delay, the reason for the delay, the defendant's assertion of the right, and the prejudice to the defendant.[166]

Because the remedy for the government's violation of the speedy trial right – dismissal – is relatively severe, courts have often hesitated to find violations of the right. However, the Supreme Court has indicated that extremely long delays violate a person's Sixth Amendment right to a speedy trial even in the absence of "affirmative proof of particularized prejudice."[167] It is possible that a court could find that some Guantanamo detainees have been prejudiced in any future prosecution by their long periods of detention, since "a defendant confined to jail prior to trial is obviously disadvantaged by delay."[168] If so, a key question in cases involving Guantanamo detainees might be whether the prejudice suffered by detainees outweighs the public's interest in delaying prosecution. However, it is possible that a court would find that non-citizen detainees were not entitled to a speedy trial right prior to their transfer to the United States,[169] which may affect a reviewing court's consideration of any speedy trial claims.

In addition to these constitutional requirements, statutes and forum rules may impose speedy trial requirements of their own. The Federal Speedy Trial Act of 1974 delineates specific speedy trial rules in the context of federal courts.[170] As a general rule, the Speedy Trial Act requires that the government bring an indictment against a person within 30 days of arrest, and that trial commences within 70 days of indictment.[171] However, the Act provides several specific exceptions, under which the determination regarding speed of prosecution becomes nearly as much a balancing act as under the Supreme Court's interpretation of the constitutional right. Potentially relevant exceptions to the prosecution of detainees permit a trial judge to grant a so-called "ends of justice" continuance if he or she determines that the continuance serves "ends of justice" that outweigh the interests of the public and defendant in a speedy trial, and also permit the granting of a continuance when the facts at issue are "unusual or complex."[172] Presumably, many of the same factors that are important in considering constitutional issues relating to a right to a speedy trial are also relevant when interpreting the statutory requirements of the Speedy Trial Act.[173]

In *United States v. al-Arian*, the United States charged four men with having provided material support to terrorists, among other charges.[174] The primary evidence in the case included more than 250 taped telephone conversations, which the U.S. government had collected pursuant to the Foreign Intelligence Surveillance Act.[175] A federal district court granted co-defendants' motion for a continuance in the case over the objection of one defendant, al-Arian, who claimed that the continuance violated his constitutional right to a speedy trial.[176] The court determined that the "ends of justice" would be served by granting the continuance because factors such as the complexity of the case, the "voluminous" discovery involved, and the "novel questions of fact and law" outweighed the defendant's interest in a speedy trial.[177] In addition, the *al-Arian* court found that the defendant had failed to prove that he would suffer any specific prejudice as a result of the continuance, because the period of the continuance would in any case be consumed with discovery proceedings.[178]

There are no statutory or procedural rule requirements governing military commissions concerning enemy combatant's right to a speedy trial. While many UCMJ requirements apply to military commission proceedings, those relating to the right to a speedy trial do not.[179] Whatever rights owed to the accused in this context are only those provided by the Sixth Amendment.

In contrast, statutory requirements and forum rules afford significant speedy trial rights to individuals subject to courts-martial. Article 10 of the UCMJ requires the government, when a person is placed in arrest or confinement prior to trial, to take immediate steps to inform of the accusations and to try the case or dismiss the charges and release.[180] The R.C.M. implements this requirement in Rule 707(a) with a requirement that an individual be brought to trial within 120 days of the preferral of charges or the imposition of restraint, whichever date is earliest.[181] Rule 707 provides for certain circumstances when time periods of delay are excluded from the 120 day requirement, as well as allows the military judge or the convening authority to exclude other periods of time.[182]

On their face, the statutory and procedural rules concerning speedy trial rights in courts-martial proceedings may pose a significant obstacle for their usage in prosecuting persons held at Guantanamo. While enemy combatants may be tried by a general court-martial for war crimes under the UCMJ,[183] statutory and procedural rules governing a defendant's right to a speedy trial may be implicated. Arguably, the speedy trial requirement may have started to run when the enemy combatants were placed in confinement by the United States military.[184] And while it is possible to exclude time from the speedy trial requirement for those periods when the accused was in the custody of civilian authorities or foreign countries,[185] it may be difficult to argue that the speedy trial period did not start when the U.S. military commenced detention of the person at Guantanamo. The government is not precluded from preferring charges to a general court-martial in this scenario, but the defense has the right to object to the trial on the basis of the speedy trial requirement.[186] Prosecution of detainees before a general courts-martial may require modification of applicable statutes and forum rules relating to a defendant's right to a speedy trial.

Finally, even if the government complied with time constraints imposed by applicable statutes and forum rules and did not violate detainees' constitutional rights to a speedy trial under the Sixth Amendment, it is possible that a court could hold that the government violated a defendant's constitutional right to a fair trial under the Fifth Amendment Due Process Clause by "caus[ing] substantial prejudice to [the detainee's] right to a fair trial," typically by intentionally stalling prosecution in a case.[187]

Right to Confront Secret Evidence

The Sixth Amendment requires that "[i]n all criminal prosecutions, the accused shall enjoy the right ... to be confronted with the witnesses against him."[188] However, in the context of prosecuting persons seized in the "war on terror," a public trial could risk disclosure of classified information. In these cases, the government is arguably placed in a difficult position, forced to choose between waiving prosecution and potentially causing damage to national security or foreign relations. This dilemma was one factor leading to the enactment of the Classified Information Procedures Act (CIPA), which formalized the procedures to be used by federal courts when faced with the potential disclosure of classified information during criminal litigation.[189] Courts-martial and military commissions also have procedures concerning a defendant's right to confront secret evidence.[190]

Prosecutions implicating classified information can be factually varied, but an important distinction that may be made among them is from whom information is being kept. In some situations, the defendant seeks to introduce classified information he already has as part of his defense, and the interests of national security require sequestration of that information from the general public.[191] However, in the case of terrorism prosecutions, the more typical situation is likely to be the introduction of classified information as part of the prosecution's case against the defendant. In these cases, preventing disclosure to the defendant, as well as to the public, may be required. To that end, both CIPA and the Federal Rules of Criminal Procedure (FED. R. CRIM. P.) authorize federal courts to issue protective orders preventing disclosure of classified information to various parties, including the defendant, in cases where nondisclosure would not unduly prejudice the rights of the accused.[192]

Legal issues related to withholding classified information from a defendant are likely to arise during two distinct phases of criminal litigation. First, issues may arise during the discovery phase when the defendant requests and is entitled to classified information in the possession of the prosecution. Secondly, issues may arise during the trial phase, when classified information is sought to be presented to the trier-of-fact as evidence of the defendant's guilt. The issues implicated during both of these phases are discussed below.

Withholding Classified Information during Discovery

The mechanics of discovery in federal criminal litigation are governed primarily by the FED. R. CRIM. P. These rules provide the means by which defendants may request information and evidence in the possession of the prosecution, in many cases prior to trial. There are two important classes of information that the prosecution must provide, if requested by the defendant: specifically *Brady* material and *Jencks* material.

Brady material, named after the seminal Supreme Court case *Brady v. Maryland*,[193] refers to information in the prosecution's possession which is exculpatory, or tends to prove the innocence of the defendant. For example, statements by witnesses that contradict or are inconsistent with the prosecution's theory of the case must be provided to the defense, even if the prosecution does not intend to call those witnesses. Prosecutors are considered to have possession of information that is in the control of agencies that are "closely aligned with the prosecution,"[194] but, whether information held exclusively by elements of the intelligence community could fall within this category does not appear to have been addressed.[195]

Jencks material refers to written statements made by a prosecution witness that has testified or may testify. For example, this would include a report made by a witness called against the defendant. In the Supreme Court's opinion in *Jencks v. United States*,[196] the Court noted the high impeachment value a witness' prior statements can have, both to show inconsistency or incompleteness of the in court testimony. Subsequently, this requirement was codified by the Jencks Act.[197]

The operation of *Jencks* and *Brady* may differ significantly in the context of classified information. Under § 4 of CIPA, which deals with disclosure of discoverable classified information, the prosecution may request to submit either a redacted version or a substitute of the classified information in order to prevent harm to national security.[198] While the court may reject the redacted version or substitute as an insufficient proxy for the original, this decision is made *ex parte* without defense counsels' input or knowledge. Classified information that is also *Jencks* or *Brady* material is still subject to CIPA.[199]

In some cases, the issue may not be the disclosure of a document or statement, but whether to grant the defendant pre-trial access to government witnesses. In *United States v. Moussaoui*, one issue was the ability of the defendant to depose "enemy combatant" witnesses that were, at the time the deposition was ordered, considered intelligence assets by the United States.[200] Under the FED. R. CRIM. P., a defendant may request a deposition in order to preserve testimony at trial.[201] In *Moussaoui*, the court had determined that a deposition of the witnesses by the defendant was warranted because the witnesses had information that could have been exculpatory or could have disqualified the defendant for the death penalty.[202] However, the government refused to produce the deponents citing national security concerns.[203]

In light of this refusal, the Fourth Circuit, noting the conflict between the government's duty to comply with the court's discovery orders and the need to protect national security, considered whether the defendant could be provided with an adequate substitute for the depositions. The court also noted that substitutes would necessarily be different from depositions, and that these differences should not automatically render the substitutes inadequate.[204] Instead, the appropriate standard was whether the substitutes put the defendant in substantially the same position he would have been absent the government's national security concerns.[205] Here, the Fourth Circuit seemed to indicate that government-produced summaries of the witnesses' statements, with some procedural modifications, could be adequate substitutes for depositions.[206]

Within the courts-martial framework, the use of and potential disclosure of classified information is addressed in MIL. R. EVID. 505. The Rule applies at all stages of proceedings, including during discovery.[207] Under the Rule, the convening authority may (1) delete specified items of classified information from documents made available to the accused; (2) substitute a portion or summary of the information; (3) substitute a statement admitting relevant facts that the classified materials would tend to prove; (4) provide the document subject to conditions that will guard against the compromise of the information disclosed to the accused; or (5) withhold disclosure if actions under (1) through (4) cannot be taken without causing identifiable damage to the national security.[208] Prior to arraignment, any party may move for a pretrial session to consider matters related to classified information that may arise in connection with the trial.[209] The military judge is required, upon request of either party or *sua sponte*, to hold a pretrial session in order to address issues related to classified information, as well as any other matters that may promote a fair and expeditious trial.[210]

Disclosure of classified information during a military commission is governed by the MIL. COMM. R. EVID. 505, which implements restrictions on the release of information to protect the national security found in the MCA.[211] Much like in courts-martial, any party may move for a pretrial session to consider matters related to classified information that may arise during the military commission proceeding.[212] However, in a departure from the rules governing courts-martial, the convening authority is replaced by the military judge with respect to the modification or substitution of classified information. The military judge, upon motion of the government, has the authority to modify and/or substitute classified evidence during discovery, and ultimately may dismiss the charges or specifications with or without prejudice if he feels that the fairness of the proceeding will be compromised.[213] Additionally, when classified information is provided to the defense, modified or not, the military judge may issue a protective order to guard against the compromise of the information.[214]

The Use of Secret Evidence at Trial

The use of secret evidence at trial also implicates constitutional concerns. As described above, there may be instances where disclosure of classified information to the defendant would be damaging to the national security. In these instances, the prosecution may seek to present evidence at trial in a manner that does not result in disclosure to the defendant. One proposed scenario might be the physical exclusion of the defendant from those portions of the trial, while allowing the defendant's counsel to remain present.[215] However, such proceedings could be viewed as unconstitutionally infringing upon the defendant's Sixth Amendment right to confrontation.[216]

Historically, defendants have had the right to be present during the presentation of evidence against them, and to participate in their defense.[217] But other courts have approved of procedures which do not go so far as to require the defendant's physical presence. In *United States v. Abu Ali*, the Fourth Circuit permitted video conferences to allow the defendant to observe, and be observed by, witnesses that were being deposed in Riyadh, Saudi Arabia.[218] The Fourth Circuit stated that these procedures satisfied the Confrontation Clause if "the denial of 'face-to-face confrontation' [was] 'necessary to further an important public policy,'" and sufficient procedural protections were in place to assure the reliability of the testimony.[219] Here, the Fourth Circuit cited the protection of national security as satisfying the "important public policy" requirement. The cited procedural safeguards were the presence of mutual observation, the fact that testimony was given under oath in the Saudi criminal justice system, and the ability of defense counsel to cross examine the witnesses.[220]

Arguments alleging that protective orders violate the Confrontation Clause because they do not allow the participation of the defendant may also be undercut in the classified information context because, in some cases, the excluded defendant is not believed to have knowledge of the information being presented.[221] Therefore, his ability to provide his counsel with rebuttal information for cross examination purposes may be reduced. CIPA does not have any provisions which authorize the exclusion of defendants from any portion of trial, based upon national security considerations. But as noted earlier, CIPA § 3 authorizes the court to issue protective orders preventing disclosure of classified information to the defendant by defense counsel.

Under CIPA, the admissibility of classified information at trial is determined at a pretrial hearing. As with the case in discovery, the government may seek to replace classified information with redacted versions or substitutions. However, in this context, the adequacy of a substitute or redacted version is determined in an adversarial proceeding in which both prosecutors and defense counsel have full access to the underlying information.[222]

In the courts-martial context, MIL. R. EVID. 505 governs the use of classified information during trial. When classified material is relevant and necessary to an element of the offense or a legally cognizable defense, the convening authority may obtain the information for use by the military judge in determining how to proceed with the trial, or may dismiss the charges against the accused rather than disclose the information in the interest of protecting the national security.[223] If the classified information is provided to the judge, an *in camera proceeding* may be ordered allowing for an adversarial proceeding on the admissibility of the potential evidence.[224] Additionally, the military judge has the authority to order a protective order to prevent the disclosure of classified evidence that has been disclosed by the government to the accused.[225] In a case where classified information has not been provided to the military judge, and proceeding with the case without the information would materially prejudice a substantial right of the accused, the military judge shall dismiss the charges or specifications or both to which the classified information relates.[226]

In another departure from the rules governing courts-martial, the military judge in a military commission shall permit, upon motion of the government, the introduction of otherwise admissible evidence while protecting from disclosure the sources, methods, or activities by which the United States obtained the evidence.[227] An *in camera* presentation of classified information is also available as part of the military commission proceeding, however, the detainee may be excluded from the presentation in order to maintain the classified nature of the material and thereby protect the national security.[228] In this scenario, the detainee will not have access to the information, but his defense counsel will be able to argue the release of the information on behalf of the detainee.[229]

The MCA does not explicitly provide an opportunity for the accused to contest the admissibility of substitute evidence proffered under these procedures. It does not appear to permit the accused or his counsel to examine the evidence or a proffered substitute prior to its presentation to the military commission. If constitutional standards required by the Sixth Amendment are applicable to military commissions, the MCA may be open to challenge for affording the accused an insufficient opportunity to contest evidence. An issue may arise as to whether, where the military judge is permitted to assess the reliability of evidence based on *ex parte* communication with the prosecution, adversarial testing of the reliability of evidence before the panel members meets constitutional requirements. If the military judge's determination as to the reliability of *ex parte* evidence is conclusive, precluding entirely the opportunity of the accused to contest its reliability, the use of such evidence may serve as grounds to challenge the verdict.[230] On the other hand, if evidence resulting from classified intelligence sources and methods contains "'particularized guarantees of trustworthiness' such that adversarial testing would be expected to add little, if anything, to [its] reliability," it may be admissible and survive challenge.[231]

CONCLUSION

Since its inception, the policy of detaining suspected belligerents at Guantanamo has been the subject of controversy. In particular, there has been significant international and domestic criticism of the treatment of detainees held there, as well as detainees' limited access to federal courts by which to challenge aspects of their detention. Defenders of the policy argue that Guantanamo offers a safe and secure location away from the battlefield where suspected belligerents can be detained, and prosecuted for war crimes when appropriate. They contend that enemy belligerents should not receive the same access to federal courts as civilians within the United States.

The closure of the Guantanamo detention facility may raise complex legal issues, particularly if detainees are transferred to the United States. The nature and scope of constitutional protections owed to detainees within the United States may be different from the protections owed to those held elsewhere. The transfer of detainees into the country may also have immigration consequences.

Criminal charges could also be brought against detainees in one of several forums– i.e., federal civilian courts, the courts-martial system, or military commissions. The procedural protections afforded to the accused in each of these forums may differ, along with the types of offenses for which persons may be charged. This may affect the ability of U.S. authorities to pursue criminal charges against some detainees. Whether the military commissions established to try detainees for war crimes fulfill constitutional requirements concerning a defendant's right to a fair trial is likely to become a matter of debate, if not litigation. Legislative proposals may be considered which address these issues, though the nature of such measures may be shaped by constitutional constraints.

The issues raised by the closure of the Guantanamo detention facility have broader implications. Executive policies, legislative enactments, and judicial rulings concerning the rights and privileges owed to enemy belligerents may have long-term consequences for U.S. detention policy, both in the "war on terror" and in future armed conflicts.

Author Contact Information

Michael John Garcia
Legislative Attorney
mgarcia@crs.loc.gov, 7-3873

Edward C. Liu
Legislative Attorney
eliu@crs.loc.gov, 7-9166

Elizabeth B. Bazan
Legislative Attorney
ebazan@crs.loc.gov, 7-7202

Anna C. Henning
Legislative Attorney
ahenning@crs.loc.gov, 7-4067

R. Chuck Mason
Legislative Attorney
rcmason@crs.loc.gov, 7-9294

End Notes

[1] P.L. 107-40.

[2] Department of Defense, "Detainee Transfer Announced," press release, December 16, 2008, available at http://www.defenselink.mil/Releases/Release.aspx?ReleaseID=12394. For a detailed description of the Guantanamo detainee population, see Benjamin Wittes and Zaahira Wyne, *The Current Detainee Population of Guantánamo: AnEmpirical Study*, Brookings Institute, December 16, 2008 [hereinafter "Brookings Report"].

[3] Memorandum from the Office of Legal Counsel, Department of Justice, for William J. Haynes, General Counsel, Department of Defense, *Possible Habeas Jurisdiction over Aliens Held in Guantanamo Bay, Cuba*, December 28, 2001.

[4] *Boumediene v. Bush*, 128 S.Ct. 2229 (2008).

[5] For background, see CRS Report RL33180, *Enemy Combatant Detainees: Habeas Corpus Challenges in Federal Court*, by Jennifer K. Elsea, Michael John Garcia, and Kenneth R. Thomas; and CRS Report RL34536, *Boumediene v.Bush: Guantanamo Detainees' Right to Habeas Corpus*, by Michael John Garcia.

[6] Executive Order, "Review and Disposition of Individuals Detained at the Guantanamo Bay Naval Base and Closure of Detention Facilities," January 22, 2009, available at http://www.scotusblog.com/wp/wp-content/uploads/2009/01/guantanamo-exo-1-22-09.pdf [hereinafter "Executive Order"].

[7] *Id.* at § 4. The Order specifies that the review shall be conducted by the Attorney General (who shall also coordinatethe review process), the Secretary of Defense, the Secretary of State, the Secretary of Homeland Security, the Directorof National Intelligence, the Chairman of the Joint Chiefs of Staff, as well as other officers or full- or part-timeemployees of the U.S. government (as determined by the Attorney General, with the concurrence of the relevant department head) with intelligence, counterterrorism, military, or legal expertise.

[8] Yochi J. Dreazen, "Gates Seeks Congress's Help in Closing Guantanamo," *Wall Street Journal*, December 3, 2008.

[9] Executive Order, footnote 6, at § 4(c)(5).

[10] In the 110th Congress, a number of proposals were introduced to close the Guantanamo detention facility which contemplated the transfer of some detainees to the U.S. for trial or continued detention. *See* S. 1249, H.R. 2212, 110th Cong. (2008). Bills have also been introduced in the 111th Congress to close the facility. *See, e.g.,* S. 147, H.R. 374,111th Cong. A few non-governmental organizations have also published reports containing proposals to closeGuantanamo and transfer at least some detainees to the United States. *See* Human Rights First, *How to Close Guantanamo: Blueprint for the Next Administration*, November 2008; Sarah E. Mendelson, *Closing Guantanamo:From Bumper Sticker to Blueprint*, Center for Strategic and International Studies, September 2008.

[11] *See* DoD Press Release, footnote 2.

[12] Declaration of Joseph Benkert, Principal Deputy Assistant Secretary of Defense for Global Security Affairs, DoD, executed on June 8, 2007, at para. 3, In re Guantanamo Bay Detainee Litigation, Case No. 1:05-cv-01220 (D.D.C. 2007).

[13] *Id.*

[14] *Id.*

[15] Convention Against Torture and Other Cruel, Inhuman or Degrading Treatment or Punishment, G.A. Res. 39/46, Annex, 39 U.N. GAOR Supp. No. 51, U.N. Doc. A/39/51 (1984). CAT Article 3 requirements were implemented by the United States pursuant to the Foreign Affairs Reform and Restructuring Act of 1998, P.L. 105-277 [hereinafter "FARRA"]. For further background, see CRS Report RL32276, *The U.N. Convention Against Torture: Overview of U.S. Implementation Policy Concerning the Removal of Aliens*, by Michael John Garcia.

[16] United States Written Response to Questions Asked by the Committee Against Torture, April 28, 2006, available athttp://www.state.gov/g/drl/rls/68554.htm.

[17] Benkert Declaration, footnote 12, at para. 6.

[18] *Id.* at para. 7.

[19] For example, the United States has had negotiations with Yemen to transfer a significant number of Guantanamo detainees who are Yemeni nationals to that country. These negotiations have reportedly proven unsuccessful in part because of U.S. concerns regarding the sufficiency of Yemeni measures to minimize the threat posed by some detainees. Brookings Report, footnote 2, at 22-23; Matt Apuzzo, "'No progress' on Mass Guantanamo Prisoner Transfer," *USA Today*, July 7, 2008.

[20] *See, e.g.,* H.R. 1352, 110th Cong. (2007).

[21] 8 U.S.C. §1182(a)(3). For background, see CRS Report RL32564, *Immigration: Terrorist Grounds for Exclusion and Removal of Aliens*, by Michael John Garcia and Ruth Ellen Wasem.

[22] *See* 8 U.S.C. § 1182 (grounds for alien inadmissibility).

[23] In *Hamdi v. Rumsfeld*, 542 U. S. 507 (2004), a majority of the Supreme Court found that Congress had authorized thePresident, pursuant to the 2001 AUMF, to detain U.S. citizens properly designated as "enemy combatants" who were captured in the conflict in Afghanistan. *Id.* at 518 (O'Connor, J., plurality opinion), 588-589 (Thomas, J., dissenting). Aplurality of the Court held that even assuming that the Non-Detention Act, 18 U.S.C. § 4001(a), which limits detention of U.S. citizens except pursuant to an act of Congress, was applicable to the detention of U.S. citizens held as enemycombatants, the AUMF satisfied the Act's requirement that any detention of U.S. citizens be authorized by Congress.*Id.* at 517-518 (O'Connor, J., plurality opinion). It could be argued that the *Hamdi* plurality's reasoning supports theargument that the AUMF authorizes the President to transfer noncitizens into the United States for detention, eventhough the entry of such persons might otherwise be prohibited under the INA. On the other hand, it could be arguedthat the situation is not analogous to the facts at issue in *Hamdi.* Whereas the Non-Detention Act generally barred thedetention of U.S. citizens "except pursuant to an act of Congress," similar language is not found in the INA with respect to alien inadmissibility.

[24] *See, e.g.,* S. 108, S. 147, H.R. 374, 111th Cong (2009).

[25] 8 U.S.C. § 1182(d)(5)(A). For example, fugitives extradited to the United States whose U.S. citizenship cannot beconfirmed are paroled into the United States by immigration authorities. 7 F.A.M. 1625.6.

[26] *Leng May Ma v. Barber*, 357 U.S. 185, 189 (1958).

[27] *Hamdi*, 542 U. S. at 518 (O'Connor, J., plurality opinion), 588-589 (Thomas, J., dissenting).

[28] *Id.* at 536-537 (O'Connor, J., plurality opinion).

[29] *Id.* at 526.

[30] *al-Marri v. Pucciarelli*,534 F.3d 213 (4th Cir. 2008), *cert. granted* by 129 S.Ct. 680 (2008). *See also al-Marri v. Wright*, 487 F. 3d 160 (4th Circ. 2007). On January 22, 2009, President Obama instructed the Attorney General, Secretary of Defense, and other designated officials to review the factual and legal basis for al-Marri's continued detention as an enemy combatant, and "identify and thoroughly evaluate alternative dispositions." Memorandum from President Barack Obama to the Attorney General and Other Officials, "Review of the Detention of Ali Saleh Kahlah al-Marri," January 22, 2009, available at http://www.scotusblog.com/wp/wp-content/uploads/2009/01/obama-order-on-almarri-1-22-09.pdf. Depending upon the outcome of this review, it is possible that al-Marri could either be transferred to a foreign country or prosecuted by U.S. authorities in federal civilian court. If al-Marri is released from preventative detention, it is possible that the government will request that the Supreme Court dismiss the case as moot.

[31] 18 U.S.C. § 3142. Subject to rebuttal by the person, it is presumed that a person shall be subject to pretrial detention if the judicial officer finds there is probable cause to believe he

has committed a federal crime of terrorism for which a maximum sentence of 10 or more years' imprisonment is prescribed. *Id.* at § 3142(e).

[32] 18 U.S.C. § 3144.

[33] 8 U.S.C. § 1226. Immigration law also permits an alien to be detained for up to seven days prior to the initiation of removal proceedings or the charging of the alien with a criminal offense, if the Attorney General certifies that there are reasonable grounds to believe the alien is inadmissible or deportable on terrorism-related grounds or the alien is engaged in any other activity that endangers the national security of the United States. 8 U.S.C. § 1226a.

[34] The removal period begins on the latest of the following: (1) the date that the order of removal becomes administratively final; (2) if a reviewing court orders a stay of the removal of the alien, the date of the court's final order; or (3) if the alien is detained or confined for non-immigration purposes, the date of the alien's release. 8 U.S.C. § 1231(a)(1)(B).

[35] 8 U.S.C. § 1231(a)(2).

[36] In *Zadvydas v. Davis*, the Supreme Court concluded that the indefinite detention of deportable aliens (i.e., aliens admitted into the United States who were subsequently ordered removed) would raise significant due process concerns. The Court interpreted an applicable immigration statute governing the removal of deportable and inadmissible aliens as only permitting the detention of aliens following an order of removal for so long as is "reasonably necessary to bring about that alien's removal from the United States. It does not permit indefinite detention." *Zadyvydas v. Davis*, 533 U.S. 678, 689 (2001). The Court found that the presumptively reasonable limit for the post-removal-period detention is six months, but indicated that continued detention may be warranted when the policy is limited to specially dangerous individuals and strong procedural protections are in place. *Id.* at 690, 701. Subsequently, the Supreme Court ruled that aliens who have been paroled into the United States also could not be indefinitely detained, but the Court's holding was based on statutory construction of the applicable immigration law, and it did not consider whether such aliens were owed the same due process protections as aliens who had been legally admitted into the United States. *Clark v. Martinez*, 543 U.S. 371 (2005).

[37] 8 C.F.R. § 241.14.

[38] H.R. 6705/S. 3401, 110th Cong.

[39] The Alien Enemy Act, which was originally enacted in 1798 as part of the Alien and Sedition Act, grants the President broad authority, during a declared war or presidentially proclaimed "predatory invasion," to institute restrictions affecting alien enemies, including possible detention and deportation. 50 U.S.C. §§ 21-24. In its current form, the act applies to aliens within the United States who are fourteen years or older, and who are "natives, citizens, denizens, or subjects of the hostile nation or government" at war with the United States. 50 U.S.C. § 21. This authority was used frequently during World War I and World War II, and reviewing courts viewed such measures as constitutionally permissible. *See generally* CRS Report RL31724, *Detention of American Citizens as Enemy Combatants*, by Jennifer K. Elsea. *See also Johnson v. Eisentrager*, 339 U.S. 763, 775(1950) ("The resident enemy alien is constitutionally subject to summary arrest, internment and deportation whenever a 'declared war' exists."); *Ludecke v. Watkins,* 335 U.S. 160 (1948) (upholding President's authority to detain and remove German citizen pursuant to Alien Enemy Act). Whether more recent legal developments concerning the due process protections owed to noncitizens have come to limit this authority remains to be seen.

[40] P.L. 109-148, Title X, § 1002 (2005); P.L. 109-163, Title XIV, § 1402 (2006).

[41] *Hamdan v. Rumsfeld*, 548 U.S. 557 (2006).

[42] *Zadvydas*, 533 U.S. at 693.

[43] The application of constitutional provisions other than the Suspension Clause to noncitizens held at Guantanamo is the subject of ongoing litigation. *See Rasul v. Myers*, – S.Ct. – , 2008 WL 3910997 (U.S. Dec. 15, 2008) (vacating pre-*Boumediene* lower court judgment that aliens held at Guantanamo lacked constitutional rights under the Fifth and Eighth

Amendments, and remanding the case for further consideration in light of *Boumediene* decision).

[44] P.L. 109-148, Title X, § 1003; P.L. 109-163, Title XIV, § 1402; P.L. 109-366, § 6(c).

[45] P.L. 109-366, § 7(a). While the DTA initially stripped federal courts of jurisdiction only over claims raised by aliens held at Guantanamo, the MCA's restriction upon federal court jurisdiction applies to claims by any alien in U.S.custody who is properly detained as an enemy combatant or awaiting such a determination, regardless of the alien's location.

[46] *Boumediene*, 128 S.Ct. at 2264.

[47] *Zadvydas*, 533 U.S. at 693 ("the Due Process Clause applies to all 'persons' within the United States, including aliens, whether their presence here is lawful, unlawful, temporary or permanent").

[48] U.S. law implementing CAT generally specifies that no judicial appeal or review is available for any action, decision or claim raised under CAT, except as part of a review of a final immigration removal order. FARRA, § 2242(d). The ability of a person to raise a CAT-based claim in non-removal proceedings (e.g., in the case of extradition or military transfers), is the subject of debate and conflicting jurisprudence. *Compare Mironescu v. Costner*, 480 F.3d 664 (4th Cir. 2007), *cert. dismissed*, 128 S.Ct. 976 (U.S. Jan. 9, 2008) (finding that CAT-implementing legislation precludes review of CAT-based habeas petition in extradition proceedings); O.K. v. Bush 377 F.Supp.2d 102, n. 17 (D.D.C. 2005) (finding that CAT-based claims were not cognizable in Guantanamo transfer decisions); *with* Cornejo-Barreto v. Seifert, 218 F.3d 1004 (9th Cir. 2000) (finding that an individual subject to an extradition order may appeal under the Administrative Procedures Act (APA), when his surrender would be contrary to U.S. laws and regulations implementing CAT), disapproved in later appeal, 379 F.3d 1075 (9th Cir. 2004), opinion of later appeal vacated on rehearing by 389 F.3d 1307 (9th Cir. 2004). It should also be noted that although U.S. legislation implementing CAT required all relevant agencies to adopt regulations implementing CAT Article 3 requirements, the DoD has yet to implement such measures. It could be argued that the DoD could not transfer a detainee from the United States to a third country until CAT-implementing regulations were promulgated. *See* Robert M. Chesney, "Leaving Guantánamo: The Law of International Detainee Transfers," 40 U. Rich. L. Rev. 657 (2006) (arguing that detainees may have a right to compel the DoD to promulgate CAT-implementing regulations).

[49] 8 U.S.C. § 1158(b)(2). Members of terrorist organizations are inadmissible and ineligible for asylum. U.S. law specifies that the Taliban is a terrorist organization for INA purposes. P.L. 110-161, Div. J, § 691(d) (2007).

[50] 8 U.S.C. § 1252.

[51] Dreazen, footnote 8.

[52] *Boumediene*, 128 S.Ct. at 2258.

[53] *Zadyvdas*, 533 U.S. at 693. *See also Verdugo-Urquidez v. United States*, 494 U.S. 259, 270-71 (1990) ("aliens receive constitutional protections when they have come within the territory of the United States and developed substantial connections with the country").

[54] *See Ex Parte Quirin*, 317 U.S. 1, 25 (1942) (denying motion for leave to file writ of *habeas corpus* by eight German saboteurs tried by military commission in the United States, but noting that "Constitutional safeguards for the protection of all who are charged with offenses are not to be disregarded in order to inflict merited punishment on some who are guilty").

[55] *See, e.g., Whelchel v. McDonald*, 340 U.S. 122 (1950) ("The right to trial by jury guaranteed by the Sixth Amendment is not applicable to trials by courts-martial or military commissions."); *Quirin*, 317 U.S. at 40 ("we must conclude that § 2 of Article III and the Fifth and Sixth Amendments cannot be taken to have extended the right to demand a jury to trials by military commission, or to have required that offenses against the law of war not triable by jury at common law be tried only in the civil courts"). *See also* U.S. Const., amend. V ("No person shall be held to answer for a capital, or otherwise infamous crime,

unless on presentment or indictment of a Grand Jury, *except* in cases arising in the land or naval forces")(italics added).

[56] *Weiss v. United States*, 510 U.S. 163, 177 (1994) (upholding a narrowed interpretation of Fifth Amendment dueprocess rights for the context of military courts)(quoting *Chappell v. Wallace*, 462 U.S. 296, 301 (1983).

[57] *See* footnote 39 and accompanying citations.

[58] See generally CRS Report RL33688, *The Military Commissions Act of 2006: Analysis of Procedural Rules and Comparison with Previous DOD Rules and the Uniform Code of Military Justice*, by Jennifer K. Elsea. The MCAdefines "unlawful enemy combatant" as a person who: (1) "has engaged in hostilities or who has purposefully and materially supported hostilities against the United States or its co-belligerents who is not a lawful enemy combatant,"or (2) "has been determined to be an unlawful enemy combatant by a Combatant Status Review Tribunal or anothercompetent tribunal" by a certain date. 10 U.S.C. §948a(1). Courts have yet to rule on the constitutional legitimacy ofmany procedures used by military commissions.

[59] See Brookings Report, footnote 2, at p. 8. Information regarding ongoing and completed cases can be viewed athttp://www.defenselink.mil/news/commissions.html.

[60] *See Quirin*, 317 U.S. at 31 (upholding military commissions used to try eight German saboteurs in the United States).

[61] 10 U.S.C. § 818.

[62] *Id.*

[63] *See* 18 U.S.C. chapter 113B (terrorism-related offenses); 18 U.S.C. § 2441.

[64] *See, e.g.*, Jack L. Goldsmith and Neal Katyal, op-ed, "The Terrorists' Court," *New York Times*, July 11, 2007; Stuart Taylor, Jr., "The Case for a National Security Court," *The Atlantic*, February 27, 2008.

[65] *Chandler v. Freytag*, 348 U.S. 3, 10 (1954).

[66] *See, e.g., Gideon v. Wainwright*, 372 U.S. 335, 344 (1963); *Johnson v. Zerbst*, 304 U.S. 458, 462, 463 (1938).

[67] *Walker v. Johnston*, 312 U.S. 275 (1941).

[68] *Iowa v. Tovar*, 541 U.S. 77 (2004).

[69] *Id.*

[70] *Faretta v. California*, 422 U.S. 806 (1975). However, "under some circumstances the trial judge may deny the authority to exercise it, as when the defendant simply lacks the competence to make a knowing or intelligent waiver of counsel or when his self-representation is so disruptive of orderly procedures that the judge may curtail it." UNITED STATES CONSTITUTION: ANALYSIS AND INTERPRETATION (Constitution Annotated), found at http://crs.gov/products/conan/Amendment06/topic_8_1_7.html. *See Indiana v. Edwards*, 128 S. Ct. 2379 (2008). The right to self-representation applies only in preparation for trial and at trial. The Constitution does not guarantee a right to self-representation on direct appeal from a criminal conviction. *Martinez v. Court of App. of Cal., Fourth App. Dist.*, 528 U.S. 152, 160 (2000); *cf., Abney v. United States*, 431 U.S. 651, 656 (1977) (finding that the right to appeal, as we now know it, in criminal cases arises from statutory rather than constitutional authority. The *Martinez* Court found that it necessarily followed from this that the Sixth Amendment did not provide a basis for self-representation on appeal. 528 U.S. at 160.).

[71] *McMann v. Richardson*, 397 U.S. 759, 771 n.14 (1970); *Powell v. Alabama*, 287 U.S. 45, 71-72 (1932); *Glasser v. United States*, 315 U.S. 60, 70 (1942).

[72] *Strickland v. Washington*, 466 U.S. 668 (1984).

[73] *United States v. Cronic*, 466 U.S. 648, 658 (1984). *See also, id.* at 657-659.

[74] FED. R. CRIM. P. 44(a).

[75] 10 U.S.C. § 827.

[76] R.C.M. 506(d).

[77] R.M.C. 502(d).

[78] R.M.C. 506(c).

[79] *See, e.g.,* U.S. Congress, Senate Select Committee on Intelligence, *Current and Projected National Security Threats*, (testimony by CIA Director Michael Hayden, discussing the use of waterboarding upon three detainees currently held at Guantanamo), 110th Cong., February 5, 2008; Bob Woodward, "Detainee Tortured, Says U.S. Official," *Washington Post*, January 14, 2009, at p. A1 (quoting Susan J. Crawford, convening authority of military commissions, as stating that case of a Guantanamo detainee was not referred for prosecution because "[h]is treatment met the legal definition of torture").

[80] U.S. Const. amend. V ("No person ... shall be compelled in any criminal case to be a witness against himself, nor be deprived of life, liberty, or property, without due process of law"); U.S. Const. amend. XIV ("nor shall any statedeprive any person of life, liberty, or property, without due process of law"). *See also Malloy v. Hogan*, 378 U.S. 1, 7(1964) (incorporating the Fifth Amendment self-incrimination clause to the states). Throughout the nineteenth century, courts excluded coerced statements under a common-law rule, which arose from a judicial concern that such statementswere unreliable evidence. In *Bram v. United States*, the Supreme Court first introduced the self-incrimination clause rationale for excluding such statements. 168 U.S. 532, 542 (1887). Other twentieth century cases articulated a due-process rationale to exclude coerced statements. *See, e.g., Brown v. Mississippi*, 297 U.S. 278, 285-87 (1936) (holdingthat statements obtained by torturing an accused must be excluded under the Fourteenth Amendment due processclause, which forbids states to offend "fundamental principles of liberty and justice"). In *Miranda v. Arizona*, the Court affirmed the prominence of the *Baum* self-incrimination rationale for excluding coerced statements. 384 U.S. 436, 44445 (1966). The Court has reiterated the due-process rationale in more recent cases. *See, e.g., Dickerson v. United States*, 530 U.S. 428, 434 (2000) ("We have never abandoned [the] due process jurisprudence"). For information on more cases interpreting the Fifth Amendment right against self incrimination, see CRS Report 97-645, *Repealing Miranda?:Background of the Controversy over Pretrial Interrogation and Self-Incrimination*, by Paul Starett Wallace Jr.

[81] 384 U.S. 436, 479 (1966).

[82] *Id.* at 444. (defining questioning during "custodial interrogation" as "questioning initiated by law enforcement officers after a person has been taken into custody or otherwise deprived of his freedom of action in any significant way").

[83] *United States v. Bin Laden*, 132 F.Supp.2d 168, 173-79 (S.D.N.Y. 2001) (in a case involving a defendant who had been detained and interrogated in Kenya, holding that as a general rule, *Miranda* applies when U.S. law enforcementofficials questioned the defendant outside of the United States). This outcome seems to comport with the self-incrimination clause rationale, espoused by the *Miranda* court, for excluding coerced statements; if the concern iscompelled incrimination in a current legal proceeding, the location of the interrogation seems to be irrelevant under theconstitutional standard.

[84] In *Dickerson v. United States*, the Supreme Court held that the Miranda warnings have the status of constitutional interpretation; thus, Congress cannot eliminate the Miranda warnings requirement by statute. 530 U.S. 428, 434-435 (2000).

[85] *See, e.g., Michigan v. Tucker*, 417 U.S. 433, 444 (1974) (declining to strictly enforce the *Miranda* warnings wherepolice conduct "did not deprive respondent of his privilege against compulsory self-incrimination as such, but ratherfailed to make available to him the full measure of procedural safeguards associated with that right since *Miranda*).

[86] 467 U.S. 649 (1984).

[87] *Id.* at 655.

[88] *Id.*

[89] *Id.* at 657-58 (reasoning that requiring police to determine whether to take the time to give *Miranda* warnings "in a matter of seconds" was impracticable under the circumstances).

[90] *See, e.g.,* Jeffrey S. Becker, "Legal War on Terrorism: Extending *New York v. Quarles* and the Departure fromEnemy Combatant Designations," 53 DePaul L. Rev. 831, 869 (2003-2004).

[91] 327 F.3d 56, 145 (2d Cir. 2003), *cert. denied*, 540 U.S. 933 (2003).

[92] *Id.* at 145-46. The Fourth Circuit articulated slightly different exceptions to this general rule in *Abu Ali*, holding that *Miranda* will apply to interrogations by foreign governments when the foreign interrogators are: "(1) engaged in a joint venture with, or (2) acting as agents of, United States law enforcement officers." *Abu Ali*, 528 F.3d at 227-28.

[93] *See Abu Ali*, 528 F.3d at 232 ("When Miranda warnings are unnecessary, as in the case of an interrogation by foreign officials, we assess the voluntariness of a defendant's statements by asking whether the confession is "the product of an essentially free and unconstrained choice by its maker.") (citing *Culombe*, 367 U.S. at 602).

[94] 528 F.3d 210, 234 (4th Cir. 2008) ("[W]e conclude that Abu Ali's statements were voluntary. Abu Ali was intelligent, articulate, and comfortable with the language and culture of the country in which he was detained and questioned. The district court found, based upon copious record evidence, that he was not tortured, abused, threatened, held in cruel conditions, or subjected to coercive interrogations. On the basis of the totality of these circumstances, we conclude that Abu Ali's statements were 'the product of an essentially free and unconstrained choice.' (*citing Culombe v. Connecticut*, 367 U.S. 568, 602 (1961))).

[95] *See Dickerson*, 530 U.S. at 434 (noting that although *Miranda* and its progeny "changed the focus" of the inquiry regarding coerced statements, the Court "continue[s] to exclude confessions that were obtained involuntarily" in cases in which *Miranda* does not apply).

[96] *Hutto v. Ross*, 429 U.S. 28, 30 (1976) (citing *Bram*, 168 U.S. at 542-543).

[97] *Abu Ali*, 528 F.3d at 232.

[98] *Id.* at 233.

[99] 10 U.S.C. § 831(d). *See also* MIL. R. EVID. 305.

[100] 10 U.S.C. § 831(a),(c).

[101] *United States v. Baird*, 271 U.S. App. D.C. 121 (D.C. Cir. 1988).

[102] Not long after the passage of the UCMJ, the Court of Military Appeals (CMA) began to interpret Article 31(b) in light of congressional intent, wherein it discerned the aim on Congress's part to counteract the presumptively coercive effect created whenever a service member is questioned by a superior. *United States v. Franklin*, 8 C.M.R. 513 (C.M.A. 1952). Subsequently, the CMA determined that "person subject to the code" was not meant to be read as broadly in Article 31 as that phrase is used elsewhere in the UCMJ. *See United States v. Gibson*, 14 C.M.R. 164, 170 (C.M.A. 1954) (questioning of prisoner by fellow inmate who was cooperating with investigators did not require art. 31 warning). It has also been held that interrogation for counter- espionage purposes conducted by civilian agents of the U.S. Navy did not require an Article 31 rights warning, in a case where the suspect was found not to be in military custody at the time of the questioning. *United States v. Lonetree*, 35 M.J. 396 (C.M.A. 1992).

[103] *See* Department of the Army, AR 190-8, *Enemy Prisoners of War, Retained Personnel, Civilian Internees and Other Detainees* (1997), at para. 2-1(d). (permitting interrogation of detainees in combat zones and barring use of torture or other coercion against them, but not requiring such persons to be informed of rights under Article 31).

[104] *See* David A. Schleuter, *Military Criminal Justice* § 5-4(B) (5th ed. 1999).

[105] 10 U.S.C. § 948r(a).

[106] 10 U.S.C. § 948r(b).

[107] 10 U.S.C. § 948r(d).

[108] For further discussion, see CRS Report RL33655, *Interrogation of Detainees: Overview of the McCain Amendment*, by Michael John Garcia.

[109] 10 U.S.C. § 948r(c).

[110] 10 U.S.C. § 948r(c)-(d).

[111] *United States v. Jawad*, D-021 (November 19, 2008). The government has appealed the commission's ruling to the Court of Military Commission Review.

[112] U.S. Const., Art. I, § 10, cl. 1, prohibits the states from enacting ex post facto laws.

[113] *Stogner v. California*, 539 U.S. 607, 612 (2003), *citing Calder v. Bull*, 3 U.S. 386, 390-91 (1798). In *Calder*, Justice Chase described the Ex Post Facto Clause as four categories of laws :

> [1.]Every law that makes an action done before the passing of the law, and which was innocent when done, criminal; and punishes such action ... [2.] Every law that aggravates a crime, or makes it greater than it was, when committed ... [3.] Every law that changes the punishment, and inflicts a greater punishment, than the law annexed to the crime, when committed ... [and 4.] Every law that alters the legal rules of evidence, and receives less, or different, testimony, than the law required at the time of the commission of the offence, in order to convict the offender.
>
> *Calder*, 3 U.S. at 390-391.

[114] *See Weaver v. Graham*, 450 U.S. 24, 28 n. 10 (1981) (noting that in addition to giving protection to individuals, the Ex Post Facto Clause "upholds the separation of powers by confining the legislature to penal decisions with prospective effect and the judiciary and executive to applications of existing penal law").

[115] *Downes v. Bidwell*, 182 U.S. 244, 277 (1901). *See also United States v. Hamdan*, D012 and D050, slip op. at 2 (June 14, 2008) [hereinafter "*Hamdan* Military Commission Ruling"] (ruling by military commission citing *Downes* and finding that the Ex Post Facto Clause applies to congressional actions directed at aliens at Guantanamo).

[116] 18 U.S.C. § 2332b (acts of terrorism within the U.S. that transcend national boundaries), § 2332 (killing or severely injuring a U.S. national overseas), § 1956 (money laundering). For further discussion on the use of terrorism statutes in criminal prosecutions, including with respect to activities taking place outside the United States, see Richard B. Zabel and James J. Benjamin, Jr., *In Pursuit of Justice: Prosecuting Terrorism Cases in Federal Courts*, Human Rights First, May 2008.

[117] 18 U.S.C. § 2441.

[118] For background, see CRS Report RL31253, *Statutes of Limitation in Federal Criminal Cases: An Overview*, by Charles Doyle.

[119] *See United States v. Gorski*, 47 M.J. 370 (1997) (ruling that the Ex Post Facto Clause applies to courts-martial proceedings); *Hamdan* Military Commission Ruling, footnote 115 (finding that Ex Post Facto Clause applies tomilitary commission proceedings at Guantanamo).

[120] 10 U.S.C. § 818.

[121] *Hamdan*, 548 U.S. at 602 (Stevens, J., plurality opinion).

[122] *Id.* at 601-612 (Stevens, J., plurality opinion). Although the petitioner in *Hamdan* had been brought before a militarytribunal established by a 2001 presidential order rather than a court-martial, the Court held that UCMJ proceduralrequirements were generally applicable to these tribunals. While a majority of the Court found that the militarycommissions established by the President did not comply with these requirements, Justice Kennedy declined to join thepart of the opinion considering whether conspiracy was a cognizable offense under the law of war, finding thediscussion unnecessary in light of the Court's determination that the military commissions did not conform to the UCMJ.

[123] 10 U.S.C. § 948d(b). The military commissions established by the MCA do not have jurisdiction over "lawful enemy combatants." A "lawful enemy combatant" is defined to refer to (1) a member of the regular forces of a State party engaged in hostilities against the United States; (2) a member of a militia, volunteer corps, or organized resistancemovement belonging to a State party engaged in such hostilities, which are under responsible command, wear a fixed distinctive sign recognizable at a distance, carry their arms openly, and abide by the law of war; or (3) a member of a regular armed force who professes allegiance to a government engaged in such hostilities, but not recognized by theUnited States. 10 U.S.C. § 948a.

[124] 10 U.S.C. § 950v.

[125] 10 U.S.C. § 948d(a).

[126] 10 U.S.C. § 950p.

[127] *Hamdan*, 548 U.S. at 612 (Stevens, J., plurality opinion).

[128] For further discussion, see CRS Report RL33688, *The Military Commissions Act of 2006: Analysis of Procedural Rules and Comparison with Previous DOD Rules and the Uniform Code of Military Justice*, by Jennifer K. Elsea. The International Criminal Tribunal for the former Yugoslavia (ICTY) has found that war crimes in the context of non-international armed conflict include murder of civilians, but have implied that the killing of a combatant is not a war crime. Prosecutor v. Kvocka et al., Case No. IT-98-30/1 (Trial Chamber), November 2, 2001, para. 124: ("An additional requirement for Common Article 3 crimes under Article 3 of the Statute is that the violations must be committed against persons 'taking no active part in the hostilities.'"); Prosecutor v. Jelisic, Case No. IT-95-10 (Trial Chamber), December 14, 1999, para. 34 ("Common Article 3 protects "[p]ersons taking no active part in the hostilities" including persons "placed hors de combat by sickness, wounds, detention, or any other cause."); Prosecutor v. Blaskic, Case No. IT-95-14 (Trial Chamber), March 3, 2000, para. 180 ("Civilians within the meaning of Article 3 are persons who are not, or no longer, members of the armed forces. Civilian property covers any property that could not be legitimately considered a military objective.").

[129] *Compare Hamdan* Military Commission Ruling, footnote 115 (analogizing "material support for terrorism" to guerilla activities subject to trial by military commission in the U.S. Civil War); *with Ex Parte Milligan*, 71 U.S. (4 Wall.) 2 (1866) (citizen of Indiana accused of conspiring to commit hostile acts against the Union during Civil War, including conspiring to seize munitions stored in Union armory and liberating prisoners of war, was nevertheless a civilian who was not amenable to military jurisdiction in area where civil courts were open). Many military commissions that operated during the Civil War did not exercise jurisdiction solely over war crimes. Commissions were also used to try persons for other criminal offenses in occupied territory or in locations under conditions of martial law.

[130] U.S. Const., Art. I, § 10, cl. 8.

[131] *Hamdan*, 548 U.S. at 602 (Stevens, J., plurality opinion). *See Quirin*, 317 U.S. at 30 ("universal agreement and practice" recognized offense as violation of the law of war).

[132] *See United States v. Bin Laden*, 92 F. Supp. 2d 189, 220 (S.D.N.Y. 2000) ("provided that the acts in question are recognized by at least some members of the international community as being offenses against the law of nations, Congress arguably has the power to criminalize these acts pursuant to its power to define offenses against the law of nations"); *Hamdan* Military Commission Ruling, footnote 115

[133] *Hamdan* Military Commission Ruling, footnote 115, slip. op. at 1.

[134] *Id.*, slip op at 2-3 (conspiracy) and 3-5 (material support for terrorism).

[135] *Id.*, slip op. at 6 (quoting MCA language states that it did "not establish new crimes ... [but] are declarative of existing law," 10 U.S.C. § 950p).

[136] *Id.*, slip. op. at 5. Hamdan was subsequently convicted by the commission on the material support charge and acquited of the charge of conspiracy, and sentenced to 66 months with credit for serving all but five months. He wassubsequently transferred to his native country of Yemen in November 2008 to serve out the remainder of his sentence,and his conviction was not reviewed by a federal court. *See* Department of Defense, "Detainee Treatment Announced,"press release, November 25, 2008, available at http://www.defenselink.mil/releases/release.aspx?releaseid=12372.

[137] *Stogner*, 539 U.S. at 613-17.

[138] *Carmell v. Texas*, 529 U.S. 513, 530-31, 552; 120 S. Ct. 1620; 146 L. Ed. 2d 577 (2000); *cf.*, *Stogner*, 539 U.S. at 615-16 (dicta). In *Carmell*, the Supreme Court considered an amendment to a statute concerning certain sexual offenses which authorized conviction for such offenses based on a victim's testimony alone, in contrast to the earlier version of the statute which required the victim's testimony plus other corroborating evidence to permit conviction. The Court held that application of the amendment to conduct that occurred before the amendment's effective date violated the constitutional prohibition against ex post

facto laws. In *Stogner*, the Court found that the statute at issue was an ex post facto law, because it inflicted punishment where the defendant, by law, was not liable to any punishment. However, the Court noted in dicta, that:

. . . a statute of limitations reflects a legislative judgment that, after a certain time, no quantum of evidence is sufficient to convict. See United States v. Marion, 404 U.S. 307, 322, 30 L. Ed. 2d 468, 92 S. Ct. 455 (1971). And that judgment typically rests, in large part, upon evidentiary concerns-for example, concern that the passage of time has eroded memories or made witnesses or other evidence unavailable. ... Consequently, to resurrect a prosecution after the relevant statute of limitations has expired is to eliminate a currently existing conclusive presumption forbidding prosecution, and thereby to permit conviction on a quantum of evidence where that quantum, at the time the new law is enacted, would have been legally insufficient. And, in that sense, the new law would "violate" previous evidence-related legal rules by authorizing the courts to "'receiv[e] evidence ... which the courts of justice would not [previously have] admit[ted]'" as sufficient proof of a crime ... Nonetheless, given Justice Chase's description of the second category, we need not explore the fourth category, or other categories, further.

Id. at 615-16.

[139] *E.g. Abu Ali*, 528 F.3d at 239-240.

[140] *E.g. United States v. Moussaoui*, 382 F.3d 453, 459 (4th Cir. 2004) (noting that the government informed the court that it would not comply with the court's deposition order in case involving person accused of involvement in terrorist attacks of September 11, 2001).

[141] FED. R. EVID. 802; MIL. R. EVID. 802.

[142] FED. R. EVID. 801(D), 803; MIL. R. EVID. 801(d), 803 -804. Certain hearsay exceptions also require that the declarantbe unavailable to testify, for example, due to death or an asserted privilege.

[143] FED. R. EVID. 807; MIL. R. EVID. 807.

[144] *United States v. Rouse*, 111 F.3d 561 (8th Cir. 1997).

[145] *United States v. Dumeisi*, 424 F.3d 566 (7th Cir. 2005).

[146] FED. R. EVID. 801(D)(2)(E); MIL. R. EVID. 801(d)(2)(E).

[147] FED. R. EVID. 801(D)(2); MIL. R. EVID. 801(d)(2).

[148] MIL. COMM. R. EVID. 802-803. The proponent of the evidence may satisfy the notification requirement by providing written notice of the statement and its circumstances 30 days in advance of trial or hearing and by providing the opposing party with any materials regarding the time, place, and conditions under which the statement was produced that are in its possession.

[149] *Id.* at 803(c).

[150] *See, e.g., United States v. Coulter*, 62 M.J. 520 (2005) (applying Sixth Amendment hearsay restrictions to court-martial proceedings, including requirements of *Crawford v. Washington*, 541 U.S. 36 (2004)).

[151] In the case of *In re Yamashita*, 327 U.S. 1 (1946), the Supreme Court denied application of the writ of *habeas corpus* to a Japanese general who had been tried and convicted before a military commission in the Philippines. Having found that the Court lacked jurisdiction to review the proceedings, the Court declined to consider whether the procedures employed by the commission, which permitted significant use of hearsay evidence, violated constitutional requirements. While the Supreme Court has not definitively addressed the question of whether the Confrontation Clause applies to noncitizens at Guantanamo, the reliance on hearsay evidence in administrative determinations as to whether a detainee was an "enemy combatant" informed the Court's ruling in *Boumediene* that detainees could seek *habeas* review of the legality of their detention. 128 S.Ct. at 2268-2269. *See also Hamdan*, 548 U.S. at 638 n. 67 (Stevens, J., plurality opinion) (finding 2001 presidential order establishing military commissions violated statutory requirements concerning commission procedures, and stating that "the Government suggests no circumstances in which it would be 'fair' to

convict the accused based on evidence he has not seen or heard.")(citing cf. Crawford, 541 U.S. at 49).

[152] *Crawford v. Washington*, 541 U.S. 36 (2004). This constitutional prohibition on certain types of hearsay only prohibits the admission of statements to be used *against* the defendant. For example, in the *Moussaoui* case, involving the prosecution of an individual for involvement in the 9/11 terrorist attacks, the Fourth Circuit applied *Crawford* and prohibited the government from using statements in the substitutions for testimony from certain witnesses to show the defendant's guilt. *Moussaoui*, 382 F.3d at 481-482. Exculpatory statements in the deposition substitutions, which were clearly testimonial, would have been admissible.

[153] *United States v. Udeozor*, 515 F.3d 260 (4th Cir. 2008) (citing decisions by the First, Second, Third, Fourth, Seventh, and Tenth Circuits).

[154] *See Davis v. Washington*, 547 U.S. 813, 821, 830 (2006).

[155] *Id.* at 822.

[156] *Id.* at 827-828. The statements in this case were made during a 911 call describing a contemporaneous physical assault.

[157] The character of the questioning may be relevant but does not appear to be determinative. For example, open ended questioning may still give rise to testimonial statements that would require confrontation. *Davis*, 547 U.S. at n.1.

[158] Department of Defense, "Charges Referred on Detainee al Bahlul," press release, February 26, 2008, available athttp://www.defenselink.mil/releases/release.aspx?releaseid=11718. Eighteen persons are currently facing chargesbefore a military commission, and seven other detainees had charges brought against them that were subsequentlydropped on account of evidentiary or other difficulties. Brookings Report, footnote 2, at 8.

[159] U.S. Const. amend. VI. The right applies to prosecutions in both federal and state courts, as the Supreme Court has found the right to be one of the "fundamental" constitutional rights that the Fourteenth Amendment incorporated to the states. *Klopfer v. North Carolina*, 386 U.S. 213, 226 (1967). Justifications for the right to a speedy trial include not only a concern regarding lengthy incarceration but also societal interests in resolving crimes in a timely and effective manner. *See Barker v. Wingo, Warden* 407 U.S. 514, 519 (1972) ("there is a societal interest in providing a speedy trial which exists separate from, and at times in opposition to, the rights of the accused").

[160] *United States v. Marion*, 404 U.S. 307, 313 (1971).

[161] *Id.* at 320.

[162] *See, e.g, United States v. Becker*, 53 M.J. 229 (2000).

[163] In his concurring opinion in the case of *Reid v. Covert*, in which the Supreme Court held that court-martial jurisdiction could not be constitutionally applied to civilian dependents of members of the armed forces overseas during peacetime, Justice Frankfurter wrote that:

> Trial by court-martial is constitutionally permissible only for persons who can, on a fair appraisal, be regarded as falling within the authority given to Congress under Article I to regulate the 'land and naval Forces,' and who therefore are not protected by specific provisions of Article III and the Fifth and Sixth Amendments. It is of course true that, at least regarding the right to a grand jury indictment, the Fifth Amendment is not unmindful of the demands of military discipline. Within the scope of appropriate construction, the phrase 'except in cases arising in the land or naval Forces' has been assumed also to modify the guaranties of speedy and public trial by jury.

354 U.S. 1, 42-43 (1957) (Frankfurter, J., concurring).

[164] The Sixth Amendment provides that "In all criminal prosecutions, the accused shall enjoy the right to a speedy andpublic trial.... " The constitutional right to a speedy trial has been interpreted as generally applying to courts-martial proceedings.

[165] *See Strunk*, 412 U.S. at 438.

[166] *See Barker*, 407 U.S. at 530. Courts have recognized at least three types of prejudice, including "'oppressive pretrial incarceration,' 'anxiety and concern of the accused,' and 'the

possibility that the [accused's] defense will be impaired' by dimming memories and loss of exculpatory evidence." *See Doggett v. United States*, 505 U.S. 647, 654 (1992) (citing *Barker*, 407 U.S. at 532; *Smith v. Hooey*, 393 U.S. 374, 377-379 (1969); *United States v. Ewell*, 383 U.S. 116, 120 (1966).

[167] *Doggett v. United States*, 505 U.S. 647, 657 (1992) (holding that the government's "egregious persistence in failing to prosecute" the defendant for more than eight years after an initial indictment was "clearly sufficient" to constitute a violation of the defendant's speedy trial right, despite a lack of proof that the defendant was specifically harmed by the delay).

[168] *Barker*, 407 U.S. at 527.

[169] *See Verdugo-Urquidez v. United States,* 494 U.S. 259, at 268, 270-71 (1990) (stating that "not every constitutional provision applies to governmental activity even where the United States has sovereign power" and that "aliens receive constitutional protections when they have come within the territory of the United States and developed substantial connections with the country"), *Balzac v. Porto Rico*, 258 U.S. 298 (1922) (Sixth Amendment right to jury trial inapplicable to Puerto Rico, an unincorporated U.S. territory).

[170] 18 U.S.C. § 3161. Congress passed the Speedy Trial Act shortly after the Supreme Court, in *Baker v. Wingo*, rejected a specific, judicially imposed time period. 407 U.S. at 523. The *Baker* court held that such a specific timeframe would invade the province of the legislature. *Id.* The Speedy Trial Act is just the primary statute implementing the constitutional right for defendants in federal courts. If detainees were located in another country's jurisdiction, then the government would have to comply with both the Speedy Trials Act and the Interstate Agreement on Detainers. *See* 18 U.S.C. Appendix 2, § 2, Articles III-VI.

[171] 18 U.S.C. § 3161(b),(c).

[172] 18 U.S.C. § 3161(h)(8)(A).

[173] 18 U.S.C. § 3161(h)(8)(B)(ii).

[174] 267 F. Supp.2d 1258, 1264 (M.D. Fla. 2003).

[175] *Id.* at 1260.

[176] *Id.* at 1267.

[177] *Id.* at 1264.

[178] *Id.* at 1264 n.16.

[179] 10 U.S.C. § 948b(d) (other provisions of the UCMJ specifically excluded include those related to compulsory self-incrimination and the requirement for pretrial investigation).

[180] 10 U.S.C. § 810.

[181] R.C.M. 707(a) (Preferral occurs when an individual, with personal knowledge of or has investigated the matters set forth in the charges and specifications, signs the charges and specifications under oath asserting that they are true infact to the best of that person's knowledge and belief. *See* R.C.M. 307).

[182] R.C.M. 707(c) (allowing for the exclusion of time when appellate courts have issued stays in the proceedings, the accused is absent without authority, the accused is hospitalized due to incompetence, or is otherwise in custody of the Attorney General).

[183] *Id.* at 201(f)(1)(B).

[184] 10 U.S.C. § 810.

[185] *See United States v. Cummings*, 21 M.J. 987, 988 (N.M.C.M.R. 1986) (after being notified that the accused isavailable for the immediate pickup from civilian custody, the Government has a reasonable time to arrange for transportation of the accused before the speedy trial period begins to run), U*nited States v. Reed*, 2 M.J. 64, 67 (C.M.A. 1976) (holding "the military is not accountable for periods an accused is retained in civil confinement as a result of civil offenses irrespective of whether his initial confinement was by civil or military authority"), *United States v.Stubbs*, 3 M.J. 630, 636 (N.M.C.M.R. 1977) (confinement by the U.S. military pursuant to a Status of ForcesAgreement, in order to ensure the presence of the accused at a judicial proceeding in a foreign jurisdiction, is notattributable to the Government).

186 R.C.M. 707(c)(2).

187 *Marion*, 404 U.S. at 324.

188 U.S. CONST. amend. VI (emphasis added).

189 P.L. 96-456, *codified at* 18 U.S.C. app. 3 § 1-16.

190 MIL. R. EVID. 505, MIL. COMM. R. EVID. 505

191 This situation has traditionally been called "graymail" to suggest that the defendant may be seeking to introduce classified information to force the prosecution to dismiss the charges. *See* S. REP. NO. 96-823 at 1-4.

192 18 U.S.C. app. 3 § 3; FED. R. CRIM. P. 16(d)(1).

193 *Brady v. Maryland*, 373 U.S. 83 (1963) (holding that due process requires prosecution to turn over exculpatoryevidence in its possession).

194 *United States v. Brooks*, 966 F.2d 1500, 1503 (1992).

195 *But, see United States v.Libby*, 429 F. Supp. 2d 1 (D.D.C. March 10, 2006) (holding that, on the facts of this case,the CIA was closely aligned with special prosecutor for purposes of *Brady*).

196 *Jencks v. U.S.*, 353 U.S. 657 (1957) (holding that, in a criminal prosecution, the government may not withhold documents relied upon by government witnesses, even where disclosure of those documents might damage national security interests).

197 *Codified at* 18 U.S.C. § 3500. The Jencks Act provides definitions for so-called "Jencks material" and requiresdisclosure of such material to the defense, but only after the witness has testified.

198 18 U.S.C. app. 3, § 4.

199 *See United States v. O'Hara*, 301 F.3d 563, 569 (7th Cir. 2002) (holding that *in camera* examination and redaction of purported *Brady* material by trial court was proper).

200 *United States v. Moussaoui*, 382 F.3d 453 (4th Cir. 2004). Moussaoui was prosecuted for his involvement in the conspiracy to commit the terrorist attacks of September 11, 2001. While the U.S. Court of Appeals for the Fourth Circuit held that CIPA did not apply to question of whether Moussaoui and his standby counsel would be allowed to depose to enemy combatant witnesses, *United States v. Moussaoui*, 333 F.3d 509, 514-15 (4th Cir. 2003), both the district court and the Fourth Circuit looked to CIPA for guidance when considering the question, see *Moussaoui, supra*, 382 F.3d at 471 n. 20 and accompanying text

201 FED. R. CRIM. P. 15(a). The court should permit the deposition if there are exceptional circumstances and it is in the interest of justice.

202 *Moussaoui*, 382 F.3d at 458, 473-475.

203 *Id.* at 459.

204 *Id.* at 477. 205 *Id.*

206 *Id.* at 479-483. The precise form of the deposition substitutes is unclear as significant portions of the Fourth Circuit's opinion dealing with the substitute were redacted.

207 MIL. R. EVID. 505(d).

208 *Id.*

209 MIL. R. EVID. 505(e).

210 *Id.*

211 *See* 10 U.S.C. §§ 949d(f), 949j(c).

212 MIL. COMM. R. EVID. 505(d).

213 MIL. COMM. R. EVID. 505(e)(3), (4).

214 MIL. COMM. R. EVID. 505(e)(1).

215 *See Hamdan v. Rumsfeld*, 344 F. Supp. 2d 152, 168 (D.D.C. 2004) (describing potential procedures under military commissions established by Presidential order).

216 *See Hamdan v. Rumsfeld*, 548 U.S. 557, 634 (2006) (Stevens, J., plurality opinion) (stating that "an accused must, absent disruptive conduct or consent, be present for his trial and must be privy to the evidence against him").

[217] *See, e.g., id.*; *Crawford*, 541 U.S. at 49, 124 S.Ct. 1354, 158 L.Ed.2d 177 (2004) ("It is a rule of the common law,founded on natural justice, that no man shall be prejudiced by evidence which he had not the liberty to cross examine")(internal citations omitted).

[218] *United States v. Abu Ali*, 528 F.3d 210, 239-240 (4th Cir. 2008)(*quoting Maryland v. Craig*, 497 U.S. 836, 850 (1990)). In this case the defendant, while located in the Federal courthouse in Alexandria, Va., was able to communicate with his counsel in Riyadh via telephone during breaks in the deposition or upon the request of defense counsel.

[219] *Id.* at 241-242 (citing *Maryland v. Craig*, 497 U.S. 836 (1990), in which one-way video testimony procedures were used in a prosecution for alleged child abuse).

[220] *Id. See, also, United States v. Bell*, 464 F.2d 667 (2nd Cir. 1972) (holding that exclusion of the public and thedefendant from proceedings in which testimony regarding a "hijacker profile" was presented was consistent with the Confrontation Clause).

[221] Arguably, if the defendant is already aware of the information, the need to prevent disclosure to him is lessened.

[222] 18 U.S.C. app. 3 § 6.

[223] MIL. R. EVID. 505(f).

[224] MIL. R. EVID. 505(I).

[225] MIL. R. EVID. 505(G).

[226] MIL. R. EVID. 5050(F).

[227] MIL. COMM. R. EVID. 505(E)(6).

[228] MIL. COMM. R. EVID. 505(h)(3).

[229] *Id.*

[230] *Cf.* Crane v. Kentucky, 476 U.S. 683 (1986)(evidence concerning the manner in which a confession was obtained should have been admitted as relevant to its reliability and credibility, despite court's determination that the confession was voluntary and need not be suppressed).

[231] *Cf.* Ohio v. Roberts, 448 U.S. 56, 66 (1980)(admissibility of hearsay evidence), but cf. Crawford v. Washington, 541 U.S. 36 (2004)("Admitting statements deemed reliable by a judge is fundamentally at odds with the right of confrontation.... [The Confrontation Clause] commands ... that reliability be assessed in a particular manner: by testing in the crucible of cross-examination.").

In: Closing Guantanamo - Issues and Legal... ISBN: 978-1-60741-511-4
Editor: Noah M. Claeys

Chapter 2

ENEMY COMBATANT DETAINEES: *HABEAS CORPUS* CHALLENGES IN FEDERAL COURT*

Jennifer K. Elsea, Michael John Garcia, and Kenneth R. Thomas

SUMMARY

After the U.S. Supreme Court held that U.S. courts have jurisdiction pursuant to 28 U.S.C. § 2241 to hear legal challenges on behalf of persons detained at the U.S. Naval Station in Guantanamo Bay, Cuba, in connection with the war against terrorism (*Rasul v. Bush)*, the Pentagon established administrative hearings, called "Combatant Status Review Tribunals" (CSRTs), to allow the detainees to contest their status as enemy combatants, and informed them of their right to pursue relief in federal court by seeking a writ of *habeas corpus*. Lawyers subsequently filed dozens of petitions on behalf of the detainees in the District Court for the District of Columbia, where district court judges reached inconsistentconclusions as to whether the detainees have any enforceable rights to challenge their treatment and detention.

---

* This is an edited, reformatted and augmented version of a CRS Report for Congress publication dated September 2008.

In December 2005, Congress passed the Detainee Treatment Act of 2005 (DTA) to divest the courts of jurisdiction to hear some detainees' challenges by eliminating the federal courts' statutory jurisdiction over *habeas* claims by aliens detained at Guantanamo Bay (as well as other causes of action based on their treatment or living conditions). The DTA provides instead for limited appeals of CSRT determinations or final decisions of military commissions. After the Supreme Court rejected the view that the DTA left it without jurisdiction to review a *habeas* challenge to the validity of military commissions in the case of *Hamdan v. Rumsfeld*, the 109th Congress enacted the Military Commissions Act of 2006 (MCA) (P.L. 109-366) to authorize the President to convene military commissions and to amend the DTA to further reduce access to federal courts by "alien enemy combatants," wherever held, by eliminating pending and future causes of action other than the limited review of military proceedings permitted under the DTA.

In June 2008, the Supreme Court held in the case of *Boumediene v. Bush* that aliens designated as enemy combatants and detained at Guantanamo Bay have the constitutional privilege of *habeas corpus*. The Court also found that MCA § 7, which limited judicial review of executive determinations of the petitioners' enemy combatant status, did not provide an adequate *habeas* substitute and therefore acted asan unconstitutional suspension of the writ of *habeas*. The immediate impact of the *Boumediene* decision is that detainees at Guantanamo may petition a federal district court for *habeas* review of the legality and possibly the circumstances of their detention, perhaps including challenges to the jurisdiction of military commissions. Pertinent legislation includes H.R. 267, S. 185, S. 576, S. 1547, S. 1548, H.R. 1415, H.R. 1416, H.R. 1585, H.R. 4986, H.R. 1189, H.R. 2543, H.R. 2710, H.R. 2826, S. 1249, H.R. 5658, S. 3001, S. 3002, H.R. 2212 and H.R. 6274.

INTRODUCTION

In the 2004 case *Hamdi v. Rumsfeld*,[1] a divided Supreme Court declared that "a state of war is not a blank check for the president"and ruled that persons deemed "enemy combatants" have the right to challenge their detention before a judge or other "neutral decision-maker." The Court did not decide whether the same right applies to aliens held as enemy combatants outside of the United States, but held in *Rasul v. Bush*[2] that federal courts have jurisdiction to hear *habeas* petitions by or on behalf of such detainees. The latter decision reversed the holding of the Court of Appeals for the District of Columbia Circuit, which had agreed with the Bush Administration that no U.S. court has jurisdiction to hear petitions for *habeas corpus* by or on behalf of the detainees because they are aliens and are detained outside the sovereign territory of the United States. Lawyers filed dozens of petitions on behalf of the detainees in the District Court for the District of Columbia, where judges reached conflicting conclusions as to whether the detainees have any enforceable rights to challenge their treatment and detention.

After the Supreme Court granted certiorari to hear a challenge by one of the detainees to his trial by military tribunal, Congress passed the Detainee Treatment Act of 2005 (DTA). The DTA requires uniform standards for interrogation of persons in the custody of the Department of Defense (DOD), and expressly bans cruel, inhuman, or degrading treatment of detainees in the custody of any U.S. agency. At the same time, however, it divested the courts of jurisdiction to hear challenges by those detained at Guantanamo Bay based on their treatment or living conditions. The DTA also eliminated the federal courts' statutory jurisdiction over *habeas* claims by aliens challenging their detention at Guantanamo Bay, but provided for limited appeals of status determinations made pursuant to the DOD procedures for Combatant Status Review Tribunals (CSRTs) or by military commissions.

In *Hamdan v. Rumsfeld*, decided June 29, 2006, the Supreme Court rejected the government's argument that the DTA divested it of jurisdiction to hearthatcase, and reviewed the validity of military commissions established to try suspected terrorists of violations of the law of war, pursuant to President Bush's military order. The Court did not revisit its 2004 opinion in *Hamdi v. Rumsfeld* upholding the President's authority to detain individuals in connection with antiterrorism operations, and did not resolve whether the petitioner could claim prisoner-of-war (POW) status, but held that "in undertaking to try Hamdan and subject him to criminal punishment, the Executive is bound to complywith the Rule of Law that prevails in this jurisdiction."

In response to the Court's decision, the 109th Congress enacted the Military Commissions Act of 2006 (MCA) (P.L. 109-366) to authorize the President to convene military commissions and to amend the DTA to further reduce the access of aliens in U.S. custody to federal court by expressly eliminating court jurisdiction over all pending and future causes of action other than the limited review of military proceedings permitted under the DTA. A federal district judge dismissed Hamdan's new petition for *habeas corpus* on the basis of the DTA, as amended, holding that the MCA is not a suspension of the Writ of Habeas Corpus within the meaning of the Constitution.[3] The U.S. Court of Appeals for the D.C. Circuit issued an order dismissing other detainee cases based on similar reasoning.[4] The Supreme Court initially denied the petitioners' request for review,[5] but later granted the petitioners' motion to reconsider.[6]

In the consolidated cases of *Boumediene v. Bush* and *Al Odah v. United States*,[7] decided June 12, 2008, the Supreme Court held that aliens designated as enemy combatants and detained at Guantanamo Bay have the constitutional privilege of *habeas corpus*. The Court also found that MCA § 7, which applied DTA review procedures to petitioners' claims, did not provide an adequate *habeas* substitute and therefore acted as an unconstitutional suspension of the writ of *habeas*. The immediate impact of the *Boumediene* decision is that detainees at Guantanamo may petition a federal district court for *habeas* review of the circumstances of their detention. Although the Court held that DTA review procedures were an inadequate substitute for *habeas*, it made "no judgment as to whether the CSRTs, as currently constituted, satisfy due process standards," and emphasized that "both the DTA and the CSRT process remain intact."[8] Whether these procedures violate due process standards, facially or as applied in a given case, and whether a particular detainee is being unlawfully held, are issues that will be addressed by the District Court when reviewing the *habeas* claims of Guantanamo detainees.

In the meantime, the U.S. Court of Appeals for the Fourth Circuit addressed whether it retained jurisdiction under the MCA to hear a petition on behalf of an alien arrested in the United States and detained as an enemy combatant. In 2007, the court granted *habeas* relief to a resident alien who was arrested in Illinois on criminal charges but then transferred to South Carolina and detained in military custody as an "enemy combatant."[9] While one judge on the panel dissented with respect to the holding that the detention was not authorized by Congress, all three judges on the panel agreed that the MCA did not divest it of jurisdiction to hear the petition, notwithstanding the MCA's lack of geographical limits. The government asked for, and was granted, a rehearing *en banc*.[10] On rehearing, the full circuit agreed that the jurisdictional issue had been resolved by the recent Supreme Court *Boumediene* decision, but found little agreement on the other issue presented.[11] As a result, the case is remanded to the district court for a hearing to determine whether the petitioner is properlydetainedto be an "enemy combatant." The petitioner has reportedly asked the Supreme Court to intervene.

This report provides an overview of the CSRT procedures, summarizes court cases related to the detentions and the use of military commissions, and summarizes the Detainee Treatment Act, as amended by the Military Commissions Act of 2006, analyzing its effects on detainee-related litigation in federal court. The report summarizes pending legislation and provides an analysis of relevant constitutional issues that may have some bearing on Congress's options with respect to the Guantanamo detainees.

BACKGROUND

The White House determined in February 2002 that Taliban detainees are covered under the Geneva Conventions,[12] while Al Qaeda detainees are not,[13] but that none of the detainees qualifies for the status of prisoner of war (POW).[14] The Administration deemed allof themtobe "unlawful enemy combatants," and claimed the right to detain them without trial or continue to hold them even if they are acquitted by a military tribunal. Fifteen of the detainees had been determined by the President to be subject to his military order ("MO") of November 13, 2001,[15] making them eligible for trial by military commission.[16] The Supreme Court, however, found that the procedural rules established by the Department of Defense to govern the military commissions were not established in accordance with the Uniform Code of Military Justice (UCMJ).[17] The following sections trace the judicial developments with respect to the detention of alleged enemy combatants.

Rasul v. Bush[18]

Petitioners were two Australians and twelve Kuwaitis (a petition on behalf of two U.K. citizens was mooted by their release) who were captured during hostilities in Afghanistan and were being held in military custody at the Guantanamo Bay Naval Base, Cuba. The Administration argued, and the court below had agreed, that under the 1950 Supreme Court case *Johnson v. Eisentrager*,[19] "'the privilege of litigation' does not extend to aliens in military custody who have no presence in 'any territory over which the United States is sovereign.'" The Court distinguished *Rasul* bynoting that *Eisentrager* concerned the *constitutional* right to *habeas corpus* rather than the right as implemented by statute. The *Rasul* Court did not reach the constitutional issue, but found authority for federal court jurisdiction in 28 U.S.C. § 2241, which grants courts the authority to hear applications for *habeas corpus* "within their respective jurisdictions," by any person who claims to be held "in custody in violation of the Constitution or laws or treaties of the United States."[20]

The Court also declined to read the statute to vary its geographical scope according to the citizenship of the detainee. Justice Kennedy, in a concurring opinion, would have found jurisdiction over the Guantanamo detainees based on the facts that Guantanamo is effectively a U.S. territory and is "far removed from any hostilities," and that the detainees are "being held indefinitely without the benefit of any legal proceeding to determine their status." Noting that the Writ of Habeas Corpus ("Writ") has evolved as the primary means to challenge executive detentions, especially those without trial, the Court held that jurisdiction over *habeas* petitions does not turn on sovereignty over the territory where detainees are held. Even if the *habeas* statute were presumed not to extend extraterritorially, as the government urged, the Court found that the "complete jurisdiction and control" the United States exercises under its lease with Cuba would suffice to bring the detainees within the territorial and historical scope of the Writ.

Without expressly overruling *Eisentrager*, the Court distinguished the cases at issue to find *Eisentrager* inapplicable. *Eisentrager* listed six factors that precluded those petitioners from seeking *habeas* relief: each petitioner "(a) is an enemy alien; (b) has never been or resided in the United States; (c) was captured outside of our territory and there held in military custody as a prisoner of war; (d) was tried and convicted by a Military Commission sitting outside the United States; (e) for offenses against laws of war committed outside the United States; (f) and is at all times imprisoned outside the United States."[21] The *Rasul* Court noted that the Guantanamo petitioners, in contrast, "are not nationals of countries at war with the United States, and they deny that they have engaged in or plotted acts of aggression against the United States; they have never been afforded access to any tribunal, much less charged with and convicted of wrongdoing; and for more than two years they have been imprisoned in territory over which the United States exercises exclusive jurisdiction and control."

As to the petitioners' claims based on statutes other than the *habeas* statute, which included the federal question statute[22] as well as the Alien Tort Statute,[23] the Court applied the same reasoning to conclude that nothing precluded the detainees from bringing such claims before a federal court.[24]

The Court's opinion left many questions unanswered. It did not clarify which of the *Eisentrager* (or *Rasul*) factors would control under a different set of facts.[25] The opinion did not address whether persons detained by the U.S. military abroad in locations where the United States does not exercise full jurisdiction and control would have access to U.S. courts. The *Hamdan* opinion seems to indicate that a majority of the Court regarded *Eisentrager* as a ruling denying relief on the merits rather than a ruling precluding jurisdiction altogether.[26] Under this view, it may be argued, there was no statutory bar precluding detainees in U.S. custody overseas from petitioning for *habeas* relief in U.S. courts, although it may be substantially more difficult for such prisoners to identify a statutory or constitutional infraction that would enable them to prevail on the merits.

The Court did not decide the merits of the petitions, although in a footnote the majority opined that "Petitioners' allegations — that, although they have engaged neither in combat nor in acts of terrorism against the United States, they have been held in Executive detention for more than two years in territory subject to the long-term, exclusive jurisdiction and control of the United States, without access to counsel and without being charged with any wrongdoing — unquestionably describe 'custody in violation of the Constitution or laws or treaties of the United States.'" The opinion left to lower courts such issues as whether the detentions are authorized by Congress, who may be detained and whatevidence might be adduced to determine whether a person is an enemy combatant, or whether the Geneva Conventions afford the detainees any protections. The Court did not address the extent to which Congress might alter federal court jurisdiction over detainees' *habeas* petitions, but *Boumediene* appears to foreclose the option of eliminating it completely, at least without an adequate substitute procedure. This issue is discussed more fully below.

Combatant Status Review Tribunals

In response to Supreme Court decisions in 2004 related to "enemy combatants," the Pentagon established procedures for Combatant Status Review Tribunals (CSRTs), based on the procedures the Army uses to determine POW status during traditional wars.[27] Detainees who are determined not to be enemy combatants are to be transferred to their country of citizenship or otherwise dealt with "consistent with domestic and international obligations and U.S. foreign policy."[28] CSRTs have confirmed the status of at least 520 enemy combatants. Any new detainees that might be transported to Guantanamo Bay will go before a CSRT. The CSRTs are not empowered to determine whether the enemy combatants are unlawful or lawful, which led two military commission judges to hold that CSRT determinations are inadequate to form the basis for the jurisdiction of military commissions.[29] Military commissions must now determine whether a defendant is an unlawful enemy combatant in order to assume jurisdiction.[30]

The tribunals are administrative rather than adversarial, but each detainee has an opportunity to present "reasonably available" evidence and witnesses[31] to a panel of three commissioned officers to try to demonstrate that the detainee does not meet the criteria to be designated as an "enemy combatant," defined as "an individual who was part of or supporting Taliban or al Qaida forces, or associated forces that are engaged in hostilities against the United States or its coalition partners[,] ... [including] any person who has committed a belligerent act or has directly supported hostilities in aid of enemy armed forces."[32] Each detaineeis represented by a military officer (nota member of the Judge Advocate General ("JAG") Corps)[33] and may elect to participate in the hearing or remain silent.[34] The government's evidence is presented by the recorder, who is a military officer, preferably a judge advocate.[35]

The CSRTs are not bound by the rules of evidence that would apply in court, and the government's evidence is presumed to be "genuine and accurate."[36] The government is required to present all of its relevant evidence, including evidence that tends to negate the detainee's designation, to the tribunal.[37] The CSRT is required to assess, "to the extent practicable, whether any statement derived from or relating to such detainee was obtained as a result of coercion and the probative value, if any, of any such statement."[38] Unclassified summaries of relevant evidence may be provided to the detainee.[39] The detainee's personal representative may view classified information and comment on it to the tribunal to aid in its determination[40] but does not act as an advocate for the detainee.[41] If the tribunal determines that the preponderance of the evidence is insufficient to support a continued designation as "enemy combatant" and its recommendation is approved through the chain of command, the detainee will be informed of that decision upon finalization of transportation arrangements (or earlier, if the task force commander deems it appropriate).[42]

In March 2002, the Pentagon announced plans to create a separate process for periodically reviewing the status of detainees.[43] The process, similar to the CSRT process, affords persons detained at Guantánamo Bay the opportunity to present to a review board, on at least an annual basis while hostilities are ongoing, information to show that the detainee is no longer a threat or that it is in the interest of the United States and its allies to release the prisoner. If new information with a bearing on the detainee's classification as an "enemy combatant" comes to light, a new CSRT may be ordered using the same procedures as described above.[44] The detainee's State of nationality may be allowed, national security concerns permitting, to submit information on behalf of its national.

COURT CHALLENGES TO THE DETENTION POLICY

While the Supreme Court clarified in *Rasul* and *Boumediene* that the detainees have recourse to federal courts to challenge their detention, the extent to which they may enforce any rights they may have under the Geneva Conventions and other law continues to remain unclear. Prior to the enactment of the Detainee Treatment Act provisions eliminating *habeas* review, the Justice Department argued primarily that *Rasul v. Bush* merely decided the issue of jurisdiction, but that the 1950 Supreme Court decision in *Johnson v. Eisentrager*[45] remained applicable to limit the relief to which the detainees may be entitled. While more than one district judge from the D.C. Circuit agreed,[46] others did not, holding for example that detainees have the right to the assistance of an attorney.[47] One judge found that a detainee has the right to be treated as a POW until a "competent tribunal" decides otherwise,[48] but the appellate court reversed. The following sections summarize the three most important decisions prior to the enactment of the MCA, including the cases that eventually reached the Supreme Court as *Boumediene v. Bush* and *Hamdan v. Rumsfeld.* The Court of Appeals for the D.C. Circuit had ordered these cases dismissed for lack of jurisdiction on the basis of the MCA,[49] but the Supreme Court reversed in both its *Hamdan* and *Boumediene* decisions, returning the cases to the district court for consideration on the merits. Also discussed is a Fourth Circuit case involving an alien arrested in the United States and subsequently held in military custody as an enemy combatant. The petition, brought by Ali al-Marri, may reach the Supreme Court during its upcoming term. Al-Marri has also petitioned separately for relief from certain conditions of detention.[50]

Khalid v. Bush[51]

Seven detainees, all of whom had been captured outside of Afghanistan, sought relief from their detention at the Guantanamo Bay facility. U.S. District Judge Richard J. Leon agreed with the Administration that Congress, in its

Authorization to Use Military Force (AUMF),[52] granted President Bush the authority to detain foreign enemy combatants outside the United States for the duration of the war against al Qaeda and the Taliban, and that the courts have virtually no power to review the conditions under which such prisoners are held. Noting that the prisoners had been captured and detained pursuant to the President's military order,[53] Judge Leon agreed with the government that "(1) non-resident aliens detained under [such] circumstances have no rights under the Constitution; (2) no existing federal law renders their custody unlawful; (3) no legally binding treaty is applicable; and (4) international law is not binding under these circumstances."[54]

Judge Leon rejected the petitioners' contention that their arrest outside of Afghanistan and away from any active battlefield meant that they could not be "enemy combatants" within the meaning of the law of war, finding instead that the AUMF contains no geographical boundaries,[55] and gives the President virtually unlimited authority to exercise his war power wherever enemy combatants are found.[56] The circumstances behind the off-battlefield captures did, however, apparently preclude the petitioners from claiming their detentions violate the Geneva Conventions.[57] Other treaties put forth by the petitioners were found to be unavailing because of their non-self-executing nature.[58]

The court declined to evaluate whether the conditions of detention were unlawful. Judge Leon concluded that "[w]hile a state of war does not give the Presidenta 'blank check,' and the courts must have some role when individual liberty is at stake, any role must be limited when, as here, there is an ongoing armed conflict and the individuals challenging their detention are non-resident aliens."[59] He dismissed all seven petitions, ruling that "until Congress and the President act further, there is ... no viable legal theory under international law by which a federal court could issue a writ."

On appeal, the *Khalid* case was consolidated with *In re Guantanamo Detainee Cases* as *Boumediene v. Bush.*

In re Guantanamo Detainee Cases[60]

U.S. District Judge Joyce Hens Green interpreted *Rasul* more broadly, finding that the detainees do have rights under the U.S. Constitution and international treaties, and thus denied the government's motion to dismiss the eleven challenges before the court. Specifically, Judge Green held that the detainees are entitled to due process of law under the Fifth Amendment, and that the CSRT procedures do not meet that standard. Interpreting the history of Supreme Court rulings on the availability of constitutional rights in territories under the control of the American government (though not part of its sovereign territory), Judge Green concluded that the inquiry turns on the fundamental nature of the constitutional rights being asserted rather than the citizenship of the person asserting them. Accepting that the right not to be deprived of liberty without due process of law is a fundamental constitutional right, the judge applied a balancing test to determine what process is due in light of the government's significant interest in safeguarding national security.[61] Judge Green rejected the government's stance that the CSRTs provided more than sufficient due process for the detainees. Instead, she identified two categories of defects. She objected to the CSRTs' failure to provide the detainees with access to material evidence upon which the tribunal affirmed their "enemy combatant" status and the failure to permit the assistance of counsel to compensate for the lack of access. These circumstances, she said, deprived detainees of a meaningful opportunity to challenge the evidence against them.

Second, in particular cases, the judge found that the CSRTs' handling of accusations of torture and the vague and potentially overbroad definition of "enemy combatant" could violate the due process rights of detainees. Citing detainees' statements and news reports of abuse, Judge Green noted that the possibility that evidence was obtained involuntarily from the accused or from other witnesses, whether by interrogators at Guantanamo or by foreign intelligence officials elsewhere, could make such evidence unreliable and thus constitutionally inadmissible as a basis on which to determine whether a detainee is an enemy combatant. Judge Green objected to the definition of "enemy combatant" because it appears to cover "individuals who never committed a belligerent act or who never directly supported hostilities against the U.S. or its allies." She noted that government counsel had, in response to a set of hypothetical questions, stated that the following could be treated as enemy combatants under the AUMF: "[a] little old lady in Switzerland who writes checks to what she thinks is a charity that helps orphans in Afghanistan but [what] really is a front to finance al-Qaeda activities, a person who teaches English to the son of an al Qaeda member, and a journalist who knows the location of Osama Bin Laden but refuses to disclose it to protect her source."[62] Judge Green stated that the indefinite detention of a person solely because of his contacts with individuals or organizations tied to terrorism, and not due to any direct involvement in terrorist activities, would violate due process even if such detention were found to be authorized by the AUMF.[63]

This case was consolidated with the *Khalid* decision and heard as *Boumediene v. Bush* by the D.C. Circuit Court of Appeals, and on appeal, the Supreme Court.

Hamdan v. Rumsfeld

Salim Ahmed Hamdan, who was captured in Afghanistan and is alleged to have worked for Osama Bin Laden as a bodyguard and driver, brought this challenge to the lawfulness of the Secretary of Defense's plan to try him for alleged war crimes before a military commission,[64] arguing that the military commission rules and procedures were inconsistent with the UCMJ[65] and that he had the right to be treated as a prisoner of war under the Geneva Conventions.[66] U.S. District Judge Robertson agreed, finding no inherent authority in the President as Commander-in-Chief of the Armed Forces to create such tribunals outside of the existing statutory authority, with which the military commission rules did not comply. He also concluded that the Geneva Conventions apply to the whole of the conflict in Afghanistan, including under their protections all persons detained in connection with the hostilities there,[67] and that Hamdan was thus entitled to be treated as a prisoner of war until his status was determined to be otherwise by a competent tribunal, in accordance with article 5 of the Third Geneva Convention (prisoners of war).

The D.C. Circuit Court of Appeals reversed, ruling that the Geneva Conventions are not judicially enforceable. Judge Williams wrote a concurring opinion, construing Common Article 3 to apply to any conflict with a non-state actor,[68] without regard to the geographical confinement of such a conflict within the borders of a signatory state. The Circuit Court interpreted the UCMJ language to mean that militarycommission rules have only to be consistent with those articles of theUCMJ that refer specifically to military commissions, and therefore need not be uniform with the rules that apply to courts-martial. After the appellate court decision was handed down, Congress passed the Detainee Treatment Act of 2005 (DTA),[69] which revoked federal court jurisdiction to hear *habeas corpus* petitions and other causes of action brought by Guantanamo detainees. (The provisions of the DTA are discussed in greater detail *infra*.) The Supreme Court nevertheless granted review and reversed.

Jurisdiction

Before reaching the merits of the case, the Supreme Court declined to accept the government's argument that Congress, by passing the DTA, had stripped the Court of its jurisdiction to review *habeas corpus* challenges by or on behalf of Guantanamo detainees whose petitions had already been filed.[70] The Court also declined to dismiss the appeal as urged by the government on the basis that federal courts should abstain from intervening in cases before military tribunals that have not been finally decided,[71] noting the dissimilarities between military commission trials and ordinary courts-martial of service members pursuant to procedures established by Congress.[72] The government's argument that the petitioner had no rights conferred by the Geneva Conventions that could be adjudicated in federal court likewise did not persuade the Court to dismiss the case. Regardless of whether the Geneva Conventions provide rights enforceable in Article III courts, the Court found that Congress, by incorporatingthe "law of war" into UCMJ article 21,[73] brought the Geneva Conventions within the scope of law to be applied by courts. Justice Scalia, joined by Justices Thomas and Alito, dissented, arguing that the DTA should be interpreted to preclude the Court's review.

Presidential Authority

With respect to the authority to create the military commissions, the Court held that any power to create them must flow from the Constitution and must be among those "powers granted jointly to the President and Congress in time of war."[74] It disagreed with the government's position that Congress had authorized the commissions either whenit passed the Authorization to Use Military Force (AUMF)[75] or the DTA. Although the Court assumed that the AUMF activated the President's war powers, it did not view the AUMF as expanding the President's powers beyond the authorization set forth in the UCMJ. The Court also noted that the DTA, while recognizing the existence of military commissions, does not specifically authorize them. At most, these statutes "acknowledge a general Presidential authority to convene military commissions in circumstances where justified under the 'Constitution and laws,' including the law of war."[76]

The Geneva Conventions and the Law of War

The *habeas corpus* statute permits those detained under U.S. authority to challenge their detention on the basis that it violates any statute, the Constitution, or a treaty.[77] The D.C. Circuit nevertheless held that the Geneva Conventions are never enforceable in federal courts.[78] The Supreme Court disagreed, finding the Conventions were applicable as incorporated by UCMJ Article 21, because "compliance with the law of war is the condition upon which the authority set forth in Article 21 is granted."[79] In response to the alternative holding by the court below that Hamdan, as a putative member of al Qaeda, was not entitled to any of the protections accorded by the Geneva Conventions, the Court concluded that Common Article 3 of the Geneva Conventions applies even to members of al Qaeda, according to them a minimum baseline of protections, including protection from the "passing of sentences and the carrying out of executions without previous judgment pronounced by a regularly constituted court, affording all the judicial guarantees which are recognized as indispensable by civilized peoples."[80]

While recognizing that Common Article 3 "obviously tolerates a great degree of flexibility in trying individuals captured during armed conflict," and that "its requirements are general ones, crafted to accommodate a wide variety of legal systems," the Court found that the military commissions under M.C.O. No. 1 did not meet these criteria. In particular, the military commissions did not qualify as "regularly constituted" because they deviated too far, in the Court's view, from the rules that apply to courts-martial, without a satisfactory explanation of the need for such deviation.[81] Justice Alito, joined by Justices Scalia and Thomas, dissented, arguing that the Court is bound to defer to the President's plausible interpretation of the treaty language.

Analysis

While the *Hamdan* Court declared the military commissions as constituted under the President's Military Order to be "illegal," it left open the possibility that changes to the military commission rules could cure any defects by bringing them within the law of war and conformity with the UCMJ, or by asking Congress to authorize or craft rules tailored to the "Global War on Terrorism" (GWOT). The Court did not resolve the extent to which the detainees, as aliens held outside of U.S. territory, have constitutional rights enforceable in federal court.

The decision may affect the treatment of detainees outside of their criminal trials; for example, in interrogations for intelligence purposes. Common Article 3 of the Geneva Conventions mandates that all persons taking no active part in hostilities, including those who have laid down their arms or been incapacitated by capture or injury, are to be treated humanely and protected from "violence to life and person," torture, and "outrages upon personal dignity, in particular, humiliating and degrading treatment." Insofar as these protections are incorporated in the UCMJ and other laws, it would seem the Court is ready to interpret and adjudicate them, to the extent it retains jurisdiction to do so. It is not clear how the Court views the scope of the GWOT, however, because its decisions on the merits have been limited to cases arising out of hostilities in Afghanistan.

The opinion reaffirms the holding in *Rasul v. Bush*[82] that the AUMF does not provide the President a "blank check," and, by finding in favor of a noncitizen held overseas, seems to have expanded the *Hamdi* comment that

> [w]hatever power the United States Constitution envisions for the Executive in its exchanges with other nations or with enemy organizations in times of conflict, it most assuredly envisions a role for all three branches when individual liberties are at stake.[83]

The dissenting views also relied in good measure on actions taken by Congress, seemingly repudiating the view expressed earlier by the Executive that any efforts by Congress to legislate with respect to persons captured, detained, and possibly tried in connection with the GWOT would be an unconstitutional intrusion into powers held exclusively by the President.[84] Expressly or implicitly, all eight participating Justices applied the framework set forth by Justice Jackson in his famous concurrence in the *Steel Seizures* case,[85] which accords greater deference to the President in cases involving national security where he acts with express congressional authority than when he acts alone. The differing views among the Justices seem to have been a function of their interpretation of the AUMF and other acts of Congress as condoning or limiting executive actions.[86] The Military Commissions Act of 2006 likely resolves many issues regarding the scope of authority the President may exercise; however, the constitutionality of the various measures remains to be resolved, assuming the courts retain jurisdiction to resolve them.

Al-Marri

The case of Ali Saleh Kahlah al-Marri differs significantly from cases discussed above in that the petitioner, a lawful alien resident, was arrested and is imprisoned within the United States. Al-Marri, a Qatari student, was arrested in December 2001 in Peoria, Illinois, and transported to New York City, where he was held as a material witness for the grand jury investigating the 9/11 attacks. He was later charged with financial fraud and making false statements and transferred back to Peoria. Before his case went to trial, however, he was declared an "enemy combatant" and transferred to military custody in South Carolina. Al-Marri's counsel filed a petition for *habeas corpus* challenging al-Marri's designation and detention as an "enemy combatant." The petition was eventually dismissed for lack of jurisdiction by the U.S. Court of Appeals for the Seventh Circuit,[87] and a new petition was filed in the Fourth Circuit. In March 2005, Judge Floyd agreed with the government that the detention was authorized by the AUMF and transferred the case to a federal magistrate to examine the factual allegations supporting the government's detention of the petitioner as an enemy combatant.[88] The government provided a declaration asserting that al-Marri is closely associated with al Qaeda and had been sent to the United States prior to September 11, 2001 to serve as a "sleeper agent" for al Qaeda in order to "facilitate terrorist activities and explore disrupting this country's financial system through computer hacking."[89] The magistrate judge recommended the dismissal of the petition on the basis of information the government provided, which al-Marri did not attempt to rebut and which the magistrate judge concluded was sufficient for due process purposes in line with the *Hamdi* decision.[90] The district judge adopted the magistrate judge's report and recommendations in full, rejecting the petitioner's argument that his capture away from a foreign battlefield precluded his designation as an "enemy combatant."[91]

Al-Marri appealed, and the government moved to dismiss on the basis that the MCA strips the court of jurisdiction. The petitioner asserted that Congress did not intend to deprive him of his right to *habeas* or that, alternatively, the MCA is unconstitutional. The majority avoided the constitutional question by finding that al-Marri does not meet the statutory definition as an alien who "has been determined by the United States to have been properly detained as an enemy combatant or is awaiting such determination."[92]

Turning to the merits, the majority found that al-Marri does not fall within the legal category of "enemy combatant" within the meaning of *Hamdi*, and that the government could continue to hold him only if it charges him with a crime, commences deportation proceedings, obtains a material witness warrant in connection with grand jury proceedings, or detains him for a limited time pursuant to the Patriot Act.[93] In so holding, the majority rejected the government's contention that the AUMF authorizes the President to order the military to seize and detain persons within the United States under the facts asserted by the government, or that, alternatively, the President has inherent constitutional authority to order the detention.

The government cited the *Hamdi* decision and the Fourth Circuit's decision in *Padilla v. Hanft*[94] to support its contention that al-Marri is an enemy combatant within the meaning of the AUMF and the law of war. The court, however, interpreted *Hamdi* as confirming only that "the AUMF is explicit congressional authorization for the detention of individuals in the *narrow category* ... [of] individuals who were 'part of or supporting forces hostile to the United States or coalition partners in Afghanistan and who engaged in an armed conflict against the United States there.'"[95] Likewise, Padilla, although captured in the United States, could be detained pursuant to the AUMF onlybecause he had been, prior to returning to the United States, "'armed and present in a combat zone' in Afghanistan as part of Taliban forces during the conflict there with the United States."[96] The court explained that the two cases cited by the government, *Hamdi* and *Padilla*, involved situations similar to the World War II case *Ex parte Quirin*,[97] in which the Supreme Court agreed that eight German saboteurs could be tried by military commission because they were enemy belligerents within the meaning of the law of war.[98] In contrast, al-Marri's situation was to be likened to *Ex parte Milligan*,[99] the Civil War case in which the Supreme Court held that a citizen of Indiana accused of conspiring to commit hostile acts against the Union was nevertheless a civilian who was not amenable to military jurisdiction.[100] The court concluded that enemy combatant status rests, in accordance with the law of war, on affiliation with the military arm of an enemy government in an international armed conflict.

Judge Hudson dissented, arguing that the broad language of the AUMF, which authorized the President "to use all necessary and appropriate force against those nations, *organizations, or persons* he determines" were involved in the terrorist attacks of September 11, 2001, "would certainly seem to embrace surreptitious al Qaeda agents operating within the continental United States."[101] He would have found no meaningful distinction between the present case and *Padilla*.

The government petitioned for and was granted a rehearing *en banc*.[102] On rehearing, the narrowly divided Fourth Circuit full bench rejected the earlier panel's decision in favor of the government's position that al-Marri fits the legal definition of "enemy combatant," but also reversed the district court's decision that al-Marri was not entitled to present any more evidence to refute the government's caseagainst him. Four of the judges on the panel would have retained the earlier decision, arguing that it was not within the court's power to expand the definition of "enemy combatant" beyond the law-of-war principles at the heart of the Supreme Court's *Hamdi* decision.[103] However, these four judges joined in Judge Traxler's opinion to remand for evidentiary proceedings in order "at least [to] place the burden on the Government to make an initial showing that normal due process protections are unduly burdensome and that the Rapp declaration is "the most reliable available evidence," supporting the Government's allegations before it may order al-Marri's military detention."[104]

Judge Traxler, whose opinion is controlling for the case although not joined in full by any other panel member, agreed with the four dissenting judges that the AUMF "grants the President the power to detain enemy combatants in the war against al Qaeda, including belligerents who enter our country for the purpose of committing hostile and war-like acts such as those carried out by the al Qaeda operatives on 9/11."[105] Accordingly, he would define "enemy combatant" in the GWOT to include persons who "associate themselves with al Qaeda" and travel to the United States "for the avowed purpose of further prosecuting that war on American soil, ... even though the government cannot establish that the combatant also 'took up arms on behalf of that enemy and against our country in a foreign combat zone of that war.'"[106] Under this definition, American citizens arrested in the United States could also be treated as enemy combatants under similar allegations,[107] at least if they had traveled abroad and returned for the purpose of engaging in activity related to terrorism on behalf of al Qaeda.

However, Judge Traxler did not agree that al-Marri had been afforded due process by the district court to challenge the factual basis for his designation as an enemy combatant. While recognizing that the *Hamdi* plurality had suggested that hearsay evidence might be adequate to satisfy due process requirements for proving enemy combatant status, Judge Traxler did not agree that such relaxed evidentiary standards are necessarily appropriate when dealing with a person arrested in the United States:

> Because al-Marri was seized and detained in this country,... he is entitled to habeas review by a civilian judicial court and to the due process protections granted by our Constitution, interpreted and applied in the context of the facts, interests, and burdens at hand. To determine what constitutional process al-Marri is due, the court must weigh the competing interests, and the burden-shifting scheme and relaxed evidentiary standards discussed in *Hamdi* serve as important guides in this endeavor. *Hamdi* does not, however, provide a cookie-cutter procedure appropriate for every alleged enemy-combatant, regardless of the circumstances of the alleged combatant's seizure or the actual burdens the government might face in defending the habeas petition in the normal way.[108]

Al-Marri's case will return to the district court for evidentiary hearings, unless the Supreme Court decides to grant certiorari or, perhaps, if the government ceases to detain him as an "enemy combatant."

DETAINEE TREATMENT ACT OF 2005 (DTA)

The Detainee Treatment Act of 2005 (DTA), passed after the Court's decision in *Rasul,* requires uniform standards for interrogation of persons in the custody of the Department of Defense,[109] and expressly bans cruel, inhuman, or degrading treatment of detainees in the custody of any U.S. agency.[110] The prohibited treatment is defined as that which would violate the Fifth, Eighth, and Fourteenth Amendments to the U.S. Constitution, as the Senate has interpreted "cruel, inhuman, or degrading" treatment banned by the U.N. Convention Against Torture.[111] The provision does not create a cause of action for detainees to ask a court for relief based on inconsistent treatment, and it divests thecourts of jurisdiction to hear challengesbythosedetained at Guantanamo Bay based on their treatment or living conditions.[112] It also provides a legal defense to U.S. officers and agents who may be sued or prosecuted based on their treatment or interrogation of detainees.[113] This language appears to have been added as a compromise because the Administration reportedly sought to have the Central Intelligence Agency excepted from the prohibition on cruel, inhuman and degrading treatment on the grounds that the President needs "maximum flexibility in dealing with the global war on terrorism."[114]

The DTA also includes a modified version of the "Graham-Levin Amendment,"[115] which requires the Defense Department to submit to the Armed Services and Judiciary Committees the procedural rules for determining detainees' status.[116] The amendment neither authorizes nor requires a formal status determination, but it does require that certain congressional committees be notified 30 days prior to the implementation of any changes to the rules. As initially adopted by the Senate, the amendment would have required these procedural rules to preclude evidence determined by the board or tribunal to have been obtained by undue coercion, however, the conferees modified the language so that the tribunal or board must assess, "to the extent practicable ... whether any statement derived from or relating to such detainee was obtained as a result of coercion" and "the probative value, if any, of any such statement."

The Graham-Levin Amendment also eliminated the federal courts' statutory jurisdiction over *habeas* claims by aliens detained at Guantanamo Bay, but provides for limited appeals of status determinations made pursuant to the DOD procedures for Combatant Status Review Tribunals (CSRTs). In June 2008, the Supreme Court invalidated the provision that eliminated *habeas corpus* jurisdiction, but stated that the DTA appellate process "remains intact,"[117] although it appears that the process is not an adequate substitute for *habeas* review. However, it no longer constitutes the sole avenue by which a detainee may seek judicial review of his detention, as a detainee may also seek *habeas* review by a federal district court. It appears that courts will not require detainees to exhaust their options under the DTA appeals process prior to seeking *habeas* review, at least in cases currently pending.

Under the appellate process prescribed by the DTA, the D.C. Circuit Court of Appeals has exclusive jurisdiction to hear appeals of any status determination made by a "Designated Civilian Official," but the review is limited to a consideration of whether the determination was made consistently with applicable DOD procedures, including whether it is supported by the preponderance of the evidence, but allowing a rebuttable presumption in favor of the government. The procedural rule regarding the use of evidence obtained through undue coercion applies prospectively only, so that detainees who have already been determined by CSRTs to be enemy combatants may not base an appeal on the failure to comply with that procedure. Detainees may also appeal status determinations on the basis that, "to the extent the Constitution and laws of the United States are applicable, whether the use of such standards and procedures to make the determination is consistent with the Constitution and laws of the United States." Jurisdiction was to cease if the detainee were transferred from DOD custody. (Currently, jurisdiction is cut off if the detainee is transferred from U.S. custody.)

The DTA also provides for an appeal to the Court of Appeals for the District of Columbia Circuit of final sentences rendered by a military commission. As initially enacted, the DTA required the court to review capital cases or cases in which the alien was sentenced to death or to a term of imprisonment for 10 years or more, and made review over convictions with lesser penalties discretionary. The scope of review was limited to considering whether the decision applied the correct standards consistent with Military Commission Order No. 1 (implementing the President's Military Order) and whether those standards were consistent with the Constitution and laws of the United States, to the extent applicable.

The Military Commissions Act of 2006 (MCA)

After the Court's decision in *Hamdan*, the Bush Administration proposed legislation to Congress,[118] a version of which was enacted on October 17, 2006. The Military Commissions Act of 2006 (MCA) authorized the trial of certain detainees by military commission and prescribed detailed rules to govern their procedures.[119] The MCA also amended the DTA provisions regarding appellate review and *habeas corpus* jurisdiction.

Provisions Affecting Court Jurisdiction

The MCA expanded the DTA to make its review provisions the exclusive remedy for all aliens detained as enemy combatants anywhere in the world, rather than only those housed at Guantanamo Bay, Cuba. It does not, however, require that all detainees undergo a CSRT or a military tribunal in order to continue to be confined. Thus, any aliens detained outside of Guantanamo Bay might be effectively denied access to U.S. courts, except perhaps by means of *habeas* review.

Appeals from the final decisions of military commissions continue to go to the United States Court of Appeals for the District of Columbia Circuit,[120] but are routed through a new appellate body, the Court of Military Commission Review (CMCR). CSRT determinations continue to be appealable directly to the D.C. Circuit. Review of decisions of a military commission may only concern matters of law, not fact.[121] Appeals may be based on inconsistencies with the procedures set forth by the MCA, or, to the extent applicable, the Constitution or laws of the United States.

The MCA § 7 revoked U.S. courts' jurisdiction to hear *habeas corpus* petitions by all aliens in U.S. custody as enemy combatants, including lawful enemy combatants, regardless of the place of custody. It replaced 28 U.S.C. § 2241(e), the *habeas* provision added by the DTA, with language providing that

> (1) No court, justice, or judge shall have jurisdiction to hear or consider an application for a writ of habeas corpus filed by or on behalf of an alien detained by the United States who has been determined by the United States to have been properly detained as an enemy combatant or is awaiting such determination. (2) Except as provided in paragraphs (2) [review of CSRT determinations] and (3) [review of final decisions of military commissions] of section 1005(e) of the Detainee Treatment Act of 2005 (10 U.S.C. 801 note),

> no court, justice, or judge shall have jurisdiction to hear or consider any other action against the United States or its agents relating to any aspect of the detention, transfer, treatment, trial, or conditions of confinement of an alien who is or was detained by the United States and has been determined by the United States to have been properly detained as an enemy combatant or is awaiting such determination.[122]

This amendment took effect on the date of its enactment, and applied to "all cases, without exception, pending on or after the date of [enactment] which relate to any aspect of the detention, transfer, treatment, trial, or conditions of detention of an alien detained by the United States since September 11, 2001." In *Boumediene v. Bush*, discussed *infra*, the Supreme Court held that MCA § 7 constituted an unconstitutional suspension of the writ of *habeas* corpus, and authorized Guantanamo detainees to petition federal district courts for *habeas* review of CSRT determinations of their enemy combatant status.

Under the DTA appeals provision, there is no apparent limit to the amount of time a detainee could spend awaiting a determination as to combatant status. Aliens who continue to be detained despite having been determined not to be enemy combatants are not permitted to challenge their continued detention or their treatment, nor are they able to protest their transfer to another country, for example, on the basis that they fear torture or persecution. However, these matters may be raised in *habeas* petition. The extent of relief the courts may be able to grant remains to be addressed by the courts.

Provisions Regarding the Geneva Conventions

A continuing source of dispute in the detention and treatment of detainees is the application of the Geneva Convention. As noted previously, the *habeas corpus* statute has traditionally provided for, among other things, challenges to allegedly unlawful detentions based on rights found in treaties.[123] Thus, for instance, Common Article 3 of the 1949 Geneva Conventions, which prohibits the "passing of sentences and the carrying out of executions without previous judgment pronounced by a regularlyconstituted court, affording all the judicial guarantees which arerecognized as indispensable by civilized peoples," has been used as a basis for challenging the confinement of detainees.[124]

Section 5 of the MCA, however, specifically precludes the application of the Geneva Conventions to *habeas* or other civil proceedings.[125] Further, the

MCA provides that the Geneva Conventions may not be claimed as a source of rights by an alien who is subject to military commission proceedings.[126] Rather, Congress deems thatthemilitary commission structure established by the actcomplies with the requirement under Common Article 3 of the Geneva Convention that trials be by a regularly constituted court.[127]

In addition, the act provides that the President shall have the authority to interpret the meaning of the Geneva Conventions.[128] The intended effect of this provision is unclear. While the President generally has a role in the negotiation, implementation, and domestic enforcement of treaty obligations,[129] this power does not generally extend to "interpreting" treaty obligations, a role more traditionally associated with courts.[130] In general, Congress is prohibited from exercising powers allocated to another branch of government.[131] In *United States v. Klein*,[132] the Congress passed a law designed to frustrate a finding of the Supreme Court as to the effect of a presidential pardon.[133] Similarly, a law that was specifically intended to grant the authority of the President to adjudicate or remedy treaty violations could violate the doctrine of separation of powers, as providingrelief from acts in violation of treaties is a judicial branch function.[134] Instead, what appears to be the main thrust of this language is to establish the authority of the President within the Executive Branch to issue interpretative regulations by Executive Order.[135] However, the context in which this additional authority would be needed is unclear.

One possible intent of this provision is that the President is being given the authority to "interpret" the Geneva Convention for diplomatic purposes (e.g., to define treaty obligations and encourage other countries to conform to such definitions). This interpretation seems unlikely, as the President's power in this regard is already firmly established.[136] Another possible meaning is that the President is being given the authority to apply the Geneva Conventions to particular fact situations, such as specifying what type of interrogation techniques may be lawfully applied to a particular individual suspected of being an enemy combatant. This interpretation is possible, but it is not clear how the power to "interpret" would be significant in that situation, as the MCA precludes application of the Geneva Convention in those contexts in which such interrogations would be challenged — military commissions, *habeas corpus*, or any other civil proceeding.[137]

The more likely intent of this language would be to give the President the authority to promulgate regulations prescribing standards of behavior of employees and agents of federal agencies. For instance, this language might be seen as authorizing the President to issue regulations to implement how agency personnel should comply with the Geneva Conventions, policies which might otherwise be addressed at the agency level. Thus, for instance, if the CIA had established internal procedures regarding how to perform interrogation consistent with the Geneva Convention, then this language would explicitly authorize the President to amend such procedures by Executive Order.[138] Whether the President already had such power absent this language is beyond the scope of this report.

Post-MCA Issues and Developments

Shortly after the enactment of the MCA, the government filed motions to dismiss all of the *habeas* petitions in the D.C. Circuit involving detainees at Guantanamo Bay[139] and the petition of an alien detained as an enemy combatant in a naval brig in South Carolina.[140] Legislation introduced at the end of the 109th Congress to amend the MCA did not reach the floor of either house.[141]

Possible Application to U.S. Citizens

Some observers raised concern that the MCA permits the President to detain American citizens as enemy combatants without trial.[142] The prohibition in the MCA with respect to *habeas corpus* petitions applied only to those filed by or on behalf of aliens detained by the United States as enemy combatants. However, the MCA can be read by implication to permit the detention of U.S. citizens as enemy combatants, although it does not permit their trial by military commission, which could affect their entitlement to relief using *habeas corpus* procedures.

A plurality of the Supreme Court held in 2004, in *Hamdi v. Rumsfeld*,[143] that the President has the authority to detain U.S. citizens as enemy combatants pursuant to the AUMF,[144] but that the determination of combatant status is subject to constitutional due process considerations. The *Hamdi* plurality was limited to an understanding that the phrase "enemy combatant" means an "individual who...was 'part of or supporting forces hostile to the United States or coalition partners' in Afghanistan and who 'engaged in an armed conflict against the United States' there,"[145] but left it to lower courts to flesh out a more precise definition. The U.S. Court of Appeals for the Fourth

Circuit found that the definition continued to apply to a U.S. citizenwho returned to the United States from Afghanistan and was arrested at the airport.[146] More recently, the Fourth Circuit appears to have expanded the definition of "enemy combatant" to individuals arrested in the United States on suspicion of planning to participate in terrorist acts without necessarily having engaged in hostilities in Afghanistan. (See discussion of *Al-Marri, supra.*)

In theory, the executive branch could detain a citizen as an enemy combatant and argue that the definition of "unlawful enemy combatant" provided in the MCA, which does not explicitly limit the definition to aliens and includes persons who provide material support to terror groups engaged in hostilities against the United States, should also apply to the detention authority already found by virtue of the AUMF. Constitutional due process would apply, and the citizen could petition for *habeas corpus* to challenge his detention, but under the MCA, the citizen-combatant would not be able to assert rights based on the Geneva Convention in support of his contention that he is not an enemy combatant. In that sense, U.S. citizens could be affected by the MCA even though it does not directly apply to U.S. citizens.

On the other hand, since the MCA definition for unlawful enemy combatant applies on its face only for the purposes of the new chapter 47a of Title 10, U.S. Code (providing for the trial by military commission of alien unlawful enemy combatants), it may be argued that outside of that context, the term "enemy combatant" should be understood in the ordinary sense, that is, to include only persons who participate directly in hostilities against the United States. This interpretation seems unlikely, given that it would also mean that this narrower definition of "enemy combatant" was also meant to apply in the context of the MCA's *habeas corpus* provisions, such that some aliens who fall under the jurisdiction of a military commission under the MCA would nevertheless have been able to argue that the MCA did not affect their right to petition for *habeas corpus* or pursue any other cause of action in U.S. court, a reading that does not seem consistent with Congress's probable intent. Further, it does not appear that Congress meant to apply a different definition of "enemy combatant" to persons depending on their citizenship. Congress could specify that U.S. citizens captured in the context of the "Global War on Terror" be subject to trial in U.S. court for treason or a violation of any other statute, or prescribe procedures for determining whether U.S. citizens are subject to detention as enemy combatants, if constitutional, but it has not done so.

DTA Challenges to Detention

At the same time as it was considering the *Boumediene* case, the D.C. Circuit was reviewing several challenges brought pursuant to the DTA in which detainees contested CSRT determinations that they are properly detained as "enemy combatants." The most advanced of these cases involved Haji Bismullah, who was captured in Afghanistan in 2003, and Husaifa Parhat and six other detainees, all ethnic Chinese Uighers captured in Pakistan in December 2001.

Bismullah v. Gates

At issue at this stage in the proceedings was a series of motions filed by both parties seeking to establish procedures governing access to classified information, attorneys' access to clients, and other matters. The petitioners sought to have the court adopt rules similar to what the district court had ordered when the cases were before it on petitions of habeas corpus. The government sought to establish rules restricting scope of discovery and attorney-client communication to what it viewed as the proper scope of the court's review, that is, the CSRT proceedings.

The D.C. Circuit in July 2007 issued an order rejecting the government's motion to limit the scope of the court's review to the official record of the CSRT hearings (*Bismullah I*).[147] Rather, the court decided, in order to determine whether a preponderance of evidence supported the CSRT determinations, it must have access to *all* the information a CSRT "is authorized to obtain and consider, pursuant to the procedures specified by the Secretary of Defense." The court denied the petitioners' motion for discovery, at least for the time being, stating there was no need for additional evidence to challenge a CSRT's ruling that specific evidence or a witness was not reasonably available. And, because the DTA does not authorize the court to hold a status determination invalid as "arbitrary and capricious," there was no need for it to evaluate the conduct of other detainees' CSRTs. The court also denied as unnecessary the petitioners' motion to appoint a special master.

The court also promised to enter a protective order to implement guidelines for handling classified and sensitive information and for government monitoring of attorney client written communications ("legal mail"). Again stressing its mandate under the DTA to determine whether a preponderance of the evidence supports a CSRT's status determination, the court found that counsel for the detainees, to aid in their capacity to assist the court, should be presumed to have a "need to know" all government information concerning their clients except for highly sensitive information, in which case the government could present the evidence to the court *ex parte*. The court rejected the government's proposal that would have allowed the government, rather than the court, to determine what unclassified information would be required to be kept under seal. With respect to legal mail, the court agreed to the government's proposal to have mail from attorneys to detainees reviewed by a "privilege team," composed of Department of Defense personnel not involved in the litigation, to redact information not pertinent to matters within the court's limited scope of review.

The government asked the panel to reconsider the ruling based on its belief that the order would require the government to undertake an overly burdensome search of all relevant federal agencies in order to create a new record for each detainee that would be entirely different from the record reviewed by the CSRT for that case. The court denied the request for rehearing, explaining its view that its previous order would not require a search for information that is not "reasonably available" (*Bismullah II*).[148] The court also suggested that the government might instead convene new CSRTs to reconfirm the detainees' status, this time ensuring that the relevant documents are retained for the purpose of review under the DTA. The government also objected to the requirement that it turn over classified information to the petitioners' counsel on the basis of the risk to intelligence sources and methods as well as the burden of conducting the necessary reviews to determine which information must be turned over. The court rejected the argument, pointing out that DOD regulations declare classified information to be not reasonably available where the originating agency declines to authorize its use in the CSRT process. In light of this fact, the court suggested, the burden of reviewing the information should not be as great as the government had argued.

The government then asked for an *en banc* hearing, but the D.C. Circuit, evenly divided, declined.[149] The government then sought expedited review at the Supreme Court, urging the Court to decide the cases concurrently with the *Boumediene* case, but the Court took no action on the request.[150] Instead, it granted certiorari and vacated the decision, remanding for reconsideration in light of its decision in *Boumediene*.[151] On August 22, 2008, the D.C. Circuit reinstated without explanation its decisions in *Bismullah I* and *Bismullah II*, presumably because it did not find the *Boumediene* ruling to conflict with its decisions in these cases.[152]

The D.C. Circuit's determination of how to carry outits mandate under the DTA was a matter of interest to the Supreme Court as it was considering

Boumediene, and may have had some bearing on the ultimate determination in that case that the DTA procedures are not an adequate substitute for the writ of habeas corpus. Accordingly, it may be worthwhile to review some of the shortcomings described by the dissent, the only opinion of the panel that addressed the adequacy of the DTA procedures as a substitute for *habeas corpus*. Judge Janice Rogers Brown, concurring separately in *Bismullah I*, set forth a number of issues she felt call into question the fairness of the CSRT proceedings. For example, she noted that the detainee bears the burden of proving that he is not an "enemy combatant" — a term she described as elastic in nature, even though the detainee may not be aware of the information he is expected to rebut, all without the assistance of counsel.[153] Further, the record presented to the CSRT is limited by the Executive, and the detainee's only recourse for seeking further evidence is through the DTA review process. If the detainee is successful in obtaining new evidence, his remedy appears to be a new CSRT.[154] Finally, she noted evidence that the CSRTs do not necessarily follow their own regulations regarding the collection and presentation of evidence.[155]

Parhat v. Gates

In October 2007, while the government's petition to the Supreme Court for certiorari in the *Bismullah* case was pending, the government produced to the counsel of Husaifa Parhat, one of the parties to the *Bismullah* case, a record (including both classified and unclassified material) of what was actually presented to Parhat's CSRT. Parhat subsequently filed a separate motion to the D.C. Circuit requesting review of the CSRT's determination that he was an enemy combatant. In June 2008, a three-judge panel for the D.C. Circuit ruled in the case of *Parhat v. Gates* that petitioner had been improperly deemed an "enemy combatant" by a CSRT, the first ruling of its kind by a federal court. Because the court's opinion contained classified information, only a redacted version has been released.[156]

Parhat, an ethnic Chinese Uigher captured in Pakistan in December 2001, was found to be an "enemy combatant" by the CSRT on account of his affiliation with a Uighur independence group known as the East Turkistan Islamic Movement (ETIM), which was purportedly "associated" with Al Qaeda and the Taliban and engaged in hostilities against the United States and its coalition partners. The basis for Parhat's alleged "affiliation" with the ETIM was that an ETIM leader ran a camp in Afghanistan where Parhat had lived and received military training. For his part, Parhat denied membership in the ETIM or engagement in hostilities against the United States, and claimed he traveled to Afghanistan solely to join the resistance against China, which was not alleged to have been a coalition partner of the United States.

The Circuit Court agreed with Parhat that the record before the CSRT did not support the finding that he was an "enemy combatant," as that term had been defined by the DOD, and accordingly the CSRT's determination was not supported by a "preponderance of the evidence" and "consistent with the standards and procedures specified by the Secretary of Defense for Combatant Status Review Tribunals," as required by the DTA.[157] The DOD defined an "enemy combatant" as

> an individual who was part of or supporting Taliban or al Qaida forces, or associated forces that are engaged in hostilities against the United States or its coalition partners. This includes any person who has committed a belligerent act or has directly supported hostilities in aid of enemy armed forces.[158]

Both parties agreed that for a detainee who is not a member of the Taliban or Al Qaeda to be deemed an enemy combatant under this definition, the government must demonstrate by a preponderance of the evidence that (1) the detainee was part of or supporting "forces"; (2) those forces are associated with Al Qaeda or the Taliban; and (3) the forces are engaged in hostilities against the United States or its coalition partners.[159]

The Circuit Court found that the evidence presented by the government to support the second and third elements was insufficient to support the CSRT's determination that Parhat was an enemy combatant. Most significantly, the court found that the principal evidence presented by the government regarding these elements — four government intelligence documents describing ETIM activities and the group's relationship with Al Qaeda and the Taliban — did not "provide any of the underlying reporting upon which the documents' bottom-line assertions are founded, nor any assessment of the reliability of that reporting."[160] As a result, the Circuit Court found that neither the CSRT nor the reviewing court itself were capable of assessing the reliability of the assertions made by the documents. Accordingly "those bare assertions cannot sustain the determination that Parhat is an enemy combatant,"[161] and the CSRT's designation was therefore improper. The Circuit Court stressed that it was not suggesting that hearsay evidence could never reliably be used to determine whether a person was an enemy combatant, or that the government must always submit the basis for its factual assertions to enable an assessment of its claims. However, evidence "must be presented in a form, or with sufficient additional information, that permits the [CSRT] and court to assess its reliability."[162]

Having found that the evidence considered by the CSRT was insufficient to support the designation of Parhat as an enemy combatant, the Circuit Court next turned to the question of remedy. Although Parhat urged the court to order his release or transfer to a country other than China, the court declined to grant such relief, postulating that the government might wish to hold another CSRT in which it could present additional evidence to support Parhat's designation as an enemy combatant. While acknowledging that the DTA did not expressly grant the court release authority over detainees, the court stated that there was nonetheless "a strong argument...[that release authority] is implicit in our authority to determine whether the government has sustained its burden of proving that a detainee is an enemy combatant,"[163] and indicated that it would not "countenance 'endless do-overs'" in the CSRT process.

The Circuit Court also noted that following the Supreme Court's ruling in *Boumediene,* Parhat could pursue immediate *habeas* relief in federal district court, where he would "be able to make use of the determinations we have made today regarding the decision of his CSRT, and...raise issues that we did not reach" before a court which unquestionably would have the power to order his release.[164] Parhat has also filed a *habeas* petition with the U.S. District Court for D.C., and requested that the court parole him into the United States pending the court's ruling.[165] Parhat's case, along with his motion for parole into the U.S., is currently pending.

BOUMEDIENE V. BUSH[166]

The petitioners in *Boumediene* are aliens detained at Guantanamo who sought *habeas* review of their continued detention. Rather than pursuing an appeal of their designation as enemy combatants by CSRTs using the DTA appeals process, the petitioners sought to have the district court decisions denying *habeas* review reversed on the basis that the MCA's "court-stripping"[167] provision was unconstitutional.[168] On appeal, the D.C. Circuit affirmed, holding that the MCA stripped it and all other federal courts of jurisdiction to consider petitioners' *habeas* applications. Relying upon its earlier opinion in *Al Odah v. United States*[169] and the 1950 Supreme Court case *Johnson v. Eisentrager,*[170] in which the Supreme Court found that the constitutional writ of *habeas* was not available to enemy aliens imprisoned for war crimes in post-WWII Germany, the D.C. Circuit held that the MCA's elimination of *habeas* jurisdiction did not operate as an unconstitutional suspension of the writ, because aliens held by the United States in foreign territory do not have a constitutional right to *habeas*.[171] Consequently, the court did not examine whether the DTA provides an adequate substitution for *habeas* review.

The Supreme Court initially denied the petitioners' request for review,[172] with three Justices dissenting to the denial and two Justices explaining the basis for their support.[173] In June 2007, however, the Court reversed its denial and granted certiorari to consider the consolidated cases of *Boumediene* and *Al Odah*. In a 5-4 opinion authored by Justice Kennedy, the Court reversed the D.C. Circuit and held that petitioners had a constitutional right to *habeas* that was withdrawn by the MCA in violation of the Constitution's Suspension Clause.[174]

Constitutional Right to Habeas

The petitioners in *Boumediene* argued that they possess a constitutional right to *habeas*, and that the MCA deprived them of this right in contravention of the Suspension Clause, which prohibits the suspension of the writ of *habeas* except "when in Cases of Rebellion or Invasion the public Safety may require it." The MCA did not expressly purport to be a formal suspension of the writ of *habeas*, and the government did not make such a claim to the Court. Instead, the government argued that aliens designated as enemy combatants and detained outside the *de jure* territory of the United States have no constitutional rights, including the constitutional privilege to *habeas*, and that therefore stripping the courts of jurisdiction to hear petitioners' *habeas* claims did not violate the Suspension Clause.

The Court began its analysis by surveying the history and origins of the writ of *habeas corpus*, emphasizing the importance placed on the writ for the Framers, while also characterizingits prior jurisprudence ashaving been "careful not to foreclose the possibility that the protections of the Suspension Clause have expanded along with post-1789 developments that define the present scope of the writ."[175] The Court characterized the Suspension Clause as not only a "vital instrument" for protecting individual liberty, but also a means to ensure that the judiciary branch would have, except in cases of formal suspension, "a time-tested device, the writ, to maintain the delicate balance of governance" between the branches and prevent "cyclical abuses" of the writ by the executive and legislative branches.[176] The Court stated that the separation-of-powers doctrine and the history shaping the design of the

Suspension Clause informed its interpretation of the reach and purpose of the Clause and the constitutional writ of *habeas*.

The Court found the historical record to be inconclusive for resolving whether the Framers would have understood the constitutional writ of *habeas* as extending to suspected enemy aliens held in foreign territory over which the United States exercised plenary, but not *de jure* control. Nonetheless, the Court interpreted the Suspension Clause as having full effect at Guantanamo. While the Court did not question the government's position that Cuba maintains legal sovereignty over Guantanamo under the terms of the 1903 lease giving the U.S. plenary control over the territory, it disagreed with the government's position that "at least when applied to non-citizens, the Constitution necessarily stops where *de jure* sovereignty ends."[177]

Instead, the Court characterized its prior jurisprudence as recognizing that the Constitution's extraterritorial application turns on "objective factors and practical concerns."[178] Here, the Court emphasized the functional approach taken in the *Insular Cases*, where it had assessed the availability of constitutional rights in incorporated and unincorporated territories under the control of United States.[179] Although the government argued that the Court's subsequent decision in *Eisentrager* stood for the proposition that the constitutional writ of *habeas* does not extend to enemy aliens captured and detained abroad, the Court found this reading to be overly constrained. According to the Court, interpreting the *Eisentrager* ruling in this formalistic manner would be inconsistent with the functional approach taken by the Court in other cases concerning the Constitution's extraterritorial application,[180] and would disregard the practical considerations that informed the *Eisentrager* Court's decision that the petitioners were precluded from seeking *habeas*.

Based on the language found in the *Eisentrager* decision and other cases concerning the extraterritorial application of the Constitution, the Court deemed at least three factors to be relevant in assessing the extraterritorial scope of the Suspension Clause: (1) the citizenship and status of the detainee and the adequacy of the status determination process; (2) the nature of the site where the person is seized and detained; and (3) practical obstacles inherent in resolving the prisoner's entitlement to the writ.

Applyingthis framework, the Court characterized petitioners' circumstances in the instant case as being significantly different from those of the detainees at issue in *Eisentrager*. Among other things, the Court noted that unlike the detainees in *Eisentrager*, the petitioners denied that they were enemy combatants, and the government's control of the post-WWII, occupied German territory in which the *Eisentrager* detainees were held was notnearlyas significant nor secure as its control over the territory where the petitioners are located. The Court also found that the procedural protections afforded to Guantanamo detainees in CSRT hearings are "far more limited [than those afforded to the *Eisentrager* detainees tried by military commission], and, we conclude, fall well short of the procedures and adversarial mechanisms that would eliminate the need for habeas corpus review."[181]

While acknowledging that it had never before held that noncitizens detained in another country's territory have any rights under the U.S. Constitution, the Court concluded that the case before it "lack[ed] any precise historical parallel."[182] In particular, the Court noted that the Guantanamo detainees have been held for the duration of a conflict that is already one of the longest in U.S. history, in territory that, while not technically part of the United States, is subject to complete U.S. control. Based on these factors, the Court concluded that the Suspension Clause has full effect at Guantanamo.

Adequacy of Habeas Corpus Substitute

Having decided that petitioners possessed a constitutional privilege to *habeas corpus*, the Court next assessed whether the court-stripping measure of MCA § 7 was impermissible under the Suspension Clause. Because the MCA did not purport to be a formal suspension of the writ, the question before the Court was whether Congress had provided an adequate substitute for *habeas corpus*. The government argued that the MCA complied with the Suspension Clause because it applied the DTA's review process to petitioners, which the government claimed was a constitutionally adequate *habeas* substitute.

Though the Court declined to "offer a comprehensive summary of the requisites for an adequate substitute for *habeas corpus*," it nonetheless deemed the *habeas* privilege, at minimum, as entitling a prisoner "to a meaningful opportunity to demonstrate that he is being held pursuant to 'the erroneous application or interpretation' of relevant law," and empowering a court "to order the conditional release of an individual unlawfully detained," though release need not be the exclusive remedy or appropriate in every instance where the writ is granted.[183] Additionally, the necessary scope of *habeas* review maybe broader, dependingupon "the rigor of any earlier proceedings."[184]

The Court noted that petitioners identified a myriad of alleged deficiencies in the CSRT process which limited a detainee's ability to present evidence rebutting the government's claim that he is an enemy combatant. Among other things, cited deficiencies include constraints upon the detainee's ability to find and present evidence atthe CSRT stage to challenge the government's case; the failure toprovide a detainee with assistance of counsel; limiting the detainee's access to government records other than those that are unclassified, potentially resulting in a detaineebeing unaware of critical allegations relied upon by the government to order his detention; and the fact that thedetainee's abilityto confront witnesses may be "more theoretical than real,"[185] given the minimal limitations placed upon the admission of hearsay evidence.

While the Court did not determine whether the CSRTs, as presently constituted, satisfy due process standards, it agreed with petitioners that there was "considerable risk of error in the tribunal's findings of fact."[186] "[G]iven that the consequence of error may be detention for the duration of hostilities that may last a generation or more, this is a risk too serious to ignore."[187] The Court held that for either the writ of *habeas* or an adequate substitute to function as an effective remedy for petitioners, a court conducting a collateral proceeding must have the ability to (1) correct errors in the CSRT process; (2) assess the sufficiency of the evidence against the detainee; and (3) admit and consider relevant exculpatory evidence that was not introduced in the prior proceeding.

The Court held that the DTA review process is a facially inadequate substitute for *habeas* review. It listed a number of potential constitutional infirmities in the review process, including the absence of provisions (1) empowering the D.C. Circuit to order release from detention; (2) permitting petitioners to challenge the President's authority to detain them indefinitely; (3) enabling the appellate court to review or correct the CSRT's findings of fact; and (4) permitting the detainee to present exculpatory evidence discovered after the conclusion of CSRT proceedings. As a result, the Court deemed MCA § 7's application of the DTA review process to petitioners as failing to provide an adequate substitute for *habeas*, therefore effecting an unconstitutional suspension of the writ.

In light of this conclusion, the Court held that petitioners could immediately pursue *habeas* review in federal district court, without first obtaining review of their CSRT designations from the D.C. Circuit as would otherwise be required under the DTA review process. While prior jurisprudence recognized that prisoners are generally required to exhaust alternative remedies before seeking federal *habeas* relief, the Court found that petitioners in the instant case were entitled to a prompt *habeas* hearing, given the length of their detention. The Court stressed, however, that except in cases of undue delay, federal courts should generally refrain from considering *habeas* petitions of detainees being held as enemy combatants until after the

CSRT had an opportunity to review their status. Acknowledging that the government possesses a "legitimate interest in protecting sources and methods of intelligence gathering," the Court announced that it expected courts reviewing Guantanamo detainees *habeas* claimsto use "discretion to accommodate thisinterest to the greatest extent possible," so as to avoid "widespread dissemination of classified information."[188]

Implications of Boumediene

As a result of the *Boumediene* decision, detainees currently held at Guantanamo may petition a federal district court for *habeas* review of status determinations made by a CSRT. However, the full consequences of the *Boumediene* decision are likely to be significantly broader. While the petitioners in *Boumediene* sought *habeas* review of their designation as enemy combatants, the Court's ruling that the constitutional writ of *habeas* extends to Guantanamo suggests that detainees may also seek judicial review of claims concerning unlawful conditions of treatment or confinement or to protest a planned transfer to the custody of another country.[189]

The conduct of trials before military commissions at Guantanamo may also be affected by *Boumediene*, as enemy combatants may now potentially raise constitutional arguments against their trial and conviction. Aliens convicted of war crimes before military commissions may also potentially seek *habeas* review of their designation as an enemy combatant by the CSRT, a designation that served as a legal requisite for their subsequent prosecution before a military commission.

Although the *Boumediene* Court held that DTA review procedures were an inadequate substitute for *habeas*, it made "no judgment as to whether the CSRTs, as currently constituted, satisfy due process standards," and emphasized that "both the DTA and the CSRT process remain intact."[190] Whether these procedures violate due process standards, facially or as applied in a given case, and whether a particular detainee is being unlawfully held, are issues that will be addressed by the District Court when reviewing the *habeas* claims of Guantanamo detainees.

Some 250 *habeas* petitions have been filed on behalf of Guantanamo detainees in the U.S. District Court for the District of Columbia. In the aftermath of the *Boumediene* ruling, the District Court adopted a resolution for the coordination and management of Guantanamo cases. The resolution calls for all current and future Guantanamo cases to be transferred by the judge to whom they have been assigned to Senior Judge Thomas F. Hogan, who has been designated to coordinate and manage all Guantanamo cases so that they may be "addressed as expeditiously as possible as required by the Supreme Court in *Boumediene v. Bush*...."[191] Judge Hogan is responsible for identifying and ruling on procedural issues common to the cases. The transferring judge will retain the case for all other purposes, though Judge Hogan is to confer with those judges whose cases raise common substantive issues, and he may address those issues with the consent of the transferring judge. District Court Judges Richard J. Leon and Emmet G. Sullivan have declined to transfer their cases for coordination, and it is possible that the three judges may reach differing opinions regarding issues common to their respective cases.

CONSTITUTIONAL CONSIDERATIONS AND OPTIONS FOR CONGRESS

The Supreme Court decision in *Boumediene* holding that the DTA violates the Constitution's Suspension Clause (article I, § 9, cl. 2) leaves open a number of constitutional questions regarding the scope of the Writ of Habeas Corpus and what options are open to Congress to make rules for the detention of suspected terrorists. The following sections provide a brief background of the writ of *habeas corpus* in the United States, outline some proposals for responding to the *Boumediene* holding, and discuss relevant constitutional considerations.

The Writ of Habeas Corpus (*ad subjiciendum*), also known as the Great Writ, has its origin in Fourteenth Century England.[192] It provides the means for those detained by the government to ask a court to order their warden to explain the legal authority for their detention. In the early days of the Republic, its primary use was to challenge executive detention without trial or bail, or pursuant to a ruling by a court without jurisdiction, but the writ has expanded over the years to include a variety of collateral challenges to convictions or sentences based on alleged violations of fundamental constitutional rights.[193] The *habeas* statute provides jurisdiction to hear petitions by persons claiming that they are held "in custody in violation of the Constitution or laws or treaties of the United States."[194] A court reviewing a petition for *habeas corpus* does not determine the guilt or innocence of thepetitioner; rather, it tests the legality of the detention and thecustodian's authority to detain. If the detention is not supported by law, the detainee is to be released.[195] Minor irregularities in trial procedures that do not amount to violations of fundamental constitutional rights are generally to be addressed on direct appeal.[196]

Article I, § 9, cl. 2, of the Constitution provides: "The Privilege of the Writ of Habeas Corpus shall not be suspended, unless when in Cases of Rebellion or Invasion the public Safety may require it." Given the emphasis the *Rasul* Court had placed on the distinction between the statutory and constitutional entitlement to *habeas corpus*, it might have seemed reasonable to suppose that Congress retained the power to revoke by statute what it had earlier granted without offending either the Court or the Constitution, without regard to establishing a public safety justification. However, as the *Boumediene* case demonstrates, the special status accorded the Writ by the Suspension Clause complicates matters.

The relevance of the distinction between a "statutory" and a "constitutional" privilege of habeas corpus is not entirely clear. The federal courts' power to review petitions under *habeas corpus* has historically relied on statute,[197] but it has been explained that the Constitution obligates Congress to provide "efficient means by which [the Writ] should receive life and activity."[198] While the Court has stated that "at the absolute minimum, the Suspension Clause protects the writ 'as it existed in 1789,'"[199] it has also presumed that " the Suspension Clause of the Constitution refers to the writ as it exists today, rather than as it existed in 1789."[200] The *Boumediene* Court declined to adopt a date of reference by which the constitutional scope of the writ is to be judged.[201] Accordingly, it remains unclear whether statutory enhancements of habeas review can ever be rolled back without implicating the Suspension Clause.[202] The constitutionally mandated scope of the writ may turn on the same kinds of "objective factors and practical considerations" that the Court stated would determine the territorial scope of the writ.

Under *Boumediene*, it appears that Congress's ability to revoke altogether the courts' jurisdiction over *habeas* petitions by certain classes of persons is constrained by the Constitution, but Congress has the power to impose some procedural regulations that may limit how courts consider such cases.[203] Congress also retains the option of withdrawing *habeas* jurisdiction if it provides an effective and adequate alternative means of pursuing relief.[204] The Court's opinion in *Boumediene* did not fully delineate the lower bounds of what the Court might consider as necessary either to preserve the constitutional scope of the writ or to provide an adequate substitute, but indicated that the prisoners are entitled to "a meaningful opportunity to demonstrate that [they are] being held pursuant to the erroneous application or interpretation of relevant law."[205] A more direct option to affect the outcome of *habeas* cases brought by detainees may involve enacting a clear statutory definition of who may be detained and the purpose of the detention, along with an appropriate procedure designed to distinguish those who meet the definition from those who do not. Such an approach could potentially increase certainty with respect to courts' decisions regarding whether the detention of particular alleged enemy combatants comports with statutes and treaties, although constitutionally based claims may remain less predictable.

Congress could formally suspend the writ with respect to the detainees, although it is unclear whether Congress's views regarding the requirements of publicsafetyare justiciable.[206] If they are, then a reviewing court's assessment of the constitutionality of habeas-suspending legislation would likely turn on whether Al Qaeda's terrorist attacks upon the United States qualify as a "rebellion or invasion," and whether the court finds that "the public safety" requires the suspension of the writ.

Congress might be able to impose some limitations upon judicial review of CSRT determinations if it strengthened the procedural protections afforded to detainees in CSRT status hearings. Legislation addressing some or all of the potential procedural inadequacies in the CSRT process identified in *Boumediene* might permit judicial review of CSRT determinations to be further streamlined.

Attorney General Michael Mukasey has recommended that Congress enact new legislation to eliminate the DTA appeals process and make *habeas corpus* the sole avenue for detainees to challenge their detention in civilian court, and also to eliminate challenges to conditions of confinement or transfers out of US custody. In a speech before the American Enterprise Institute on July 21, 2008,[207] General Mukasey discussed this suggestion along with five other points he feels Congress should address:

- Courts should be prohibited from ordering that an alien captured and detained abroad be brought to the United States for court proceedings, or be admitted and released into the United States.
- Procedures should be put in place to ensure that intelligence information, including sources and methods, would be protected from disclosure to terrorist suspects.
- Detainees awaiting trial by military commission should be prevented from bringing *habeas* petitions until the completion of their trials.
- Congress should reaffirm the authority to detain as enemy combatants persons who have "engaged in hostilities or purposefully supported al Qaeda, the Taliban, and associated organizations."

- Congress should establish sensible procedures for *habeas* challenges by assigning one district court exclusive jurisdiction over the cases, with one judge deciding common legal issues; byadopting"rules that strike a reasonable balance between the detainees' rights to a fair hearing ... and our national security needs ..." that would "not provide greater protection than we would provide to American citizens held as enemy combatants in this conflict"; and ensuring that court proceedings "are not permitted to interfere with the mission of our armed forces."

Other proposals that have been floated include the creation of a new national security court to authorize preventive detention of terror suspects[208] or the use of civilian or military courts to prosecute all detainees who cannot be released to their home country or another country willing to take them. Among the issues associated with prosecuting all of the detainees in civilian court is that the detainees may not have committed any crimes cognizable in federal court. Persons accused of engaging in terrorist acts (including attempts, conspiracies and the like) against the United States could likely be prosecuted,[209] but jurisdiction over offenses involving the provision of material support to a terrorist organization abroad is somewhat more limited, and for acts occurring prior to 2004, included only persons subject to the jurisdiction of the United States.[210]

Congress could also take no action and allow the courts to address the issues in the course of deciding the *habeas* petitions already docketed.

Scope of Challenges

Whether Congress enacts legislation to guide the courts or permits courts to resolve the *habeas* cases as they now stand, courts will be faced with determining the scope of the writ as it applies to detainees in Guantanamo and perhaps elsewhere. Although the *Boumediene* Court held that DTA reviewprocedures were an inadequate substitute for *habeas*, it expressly declined to assess "the content of the law that governs" the detention of aliens at Guantanamo.[211] Nonetheless, the Supreme Court identified a number of potential deficiencies in the status review process that necessitated *habeas* review of CSRT determinations, including the detainee's lack of counsel during the hearings; the presumption of validity accorded to the government's evidence; procedural and practical limitations upon the detainee's ability to present evidence rebutting the government's charges against him and to confront witnesses; potential limitations on the detainee's ability to introduce exculpatory evidence; and limitations on the detainee's ability to learn about the nature of the government's case against him to the extent that it is based upon classified evidence.[212] Whether these procedures violate due process standards, facially or as applied in a given case, and whether a particular detainee is being unlawfully held, are issues that will be addressed by the District Court when reviewing the *habeas* claims of Guantanamo detainees.

Boumediene considered challenges to the legality of detention, the issue at the heart of most of the *habeas* challenges brought by Guantanamo detainees to date. However, there are also some cases challenging the conditions under which a detainee is being held. These two categories of challenges may involve different procedural routes and the application of different constitutional rights. The extent to which Congress may limit the scope of challenges Guantanamo detainees may bring may turn on the unresolved question of which constitutional rights apply to aliens detained in territory abroad.

The Supreme Court has not directly addressed whether there must exist a judicial forum to vindicateall constitutional rights. Justice Scalia has pointed out that thereare particular cases, such as political questions cases, where all constitutional review is in effect precluded.[213] Other commentators point to sovereign immunity and the ability of the government to limit the remedies available to plaintiffs.[214] However, the Court has, in cases involving particular rights, generally found a requirement that effective judicial remedies must be available.[215] Although the extent of constitutional rights enjoyed by aliens outside the territory of the United States is subject to continuing debate, the right of aliens within the United States to liberty except when restricted in accordance with due process of law seems well established.

The Fact and Length of Detention

The DTA provides a means for challenging the validity of decisions by a CSRT that a detainee is an enemy combatant. The D.C. Circuit Court of Appeals has not fully clarified the scope of evidence it may review in reaching such a determination. The government has argued that administrative law (applicable to reviews of agency determinations) supplies the appropriate model for reviewing CSRT determinations, so that only the record of the CSRT proceedings is subject to review, and that extrinsic evidence not already part of the record should not be subject to discovery.[216] The D.C. Circuit, however, rejected that view, holding that its review must encompass all of the information a CSRT is authorized to obtain and consider.[217]

The D.C. Circuit's jurisdiction under the DTA also includes constitutional review of whether the standards and procedures utilized in the military proceedings below were consistent with the Constitution and laws of the United States. This seems to bring the scope of DTA proceedingscloser tothatwhich would be available in habeas review. However, *habeas* challenges may also permit challenges to detention not based solely on the adequacy of CSRT procedures. First, there is no statutory requirement that all detainees receive a CSRT determination in order to be detained, nor that detainees receive any kind of a hearing within any certain period of time after their capture. This might have left some detainees without effective means to pursue a DTA challenge. Moreover, it appears that some detainees who were determined by CSRTs to be properly classified as enemy combatants have been released from Guantanamo without a new determination, which may call into question the importance of the CSRT procedure as the primary means for obtaining release and therefore, the sole focus of a collateral challenge. Detainees may also be transferred or released based on the results of periodic reviews conducted by Administrative Review Boards (ARBs)[218] to determine whether the detainee is no longer a threat or that it is in the interest of the United States and its allies to release the prisoner. There is no opportunity under the DTA to appeal the result of an ARB finding. While new evidence uncovered by this process may result in the convening of a new CSRT to determine continued enemy combatant status,[219] the DTA does not provide an avenue to appeal a decision not to convene a new CSRT.[220] The Supreme Court's ruling that the constitutional writ of *habeas* extends to Guantanamo suggests that detainees may seek *habeas* review in such cases.

Conditions of Detention

Although it appears less common for challenges to prison conditions to be entertained under *habeas* review, such cases have been heard by federal courts on *habeas* petitions.[221] Prisoners in federal prison may also ask a district court to address such complaints using their general jurisdiction to consider claims that arise under the Constitution,[222] by means of a writ of mandamus.[223] These writs, which are directed against government officials, have been used to require those officials to act in compliance with constitutional requirements. Although these challenges are often denied on the merits or on procedural grounds, cases have been brought based on the First Amendment,[224] Sixth Amendment,[225] Eighth Amendment[226] and various other grounds.[227]

The *Boumediene* Court declined to discuss whether challenges to conditions of detention are within the constitutional scope of the writ as it applies to Guantanamo detainees.[228] A variety of challenges has been raised by detainees in Guantanamo regarding conditions of their detention, including such issues as whether prisoners can be held in solitary confinement[229] when they can be transferred,[230] or whether they can have contact with relatives.[231] Although some of these were brought as *habeas corpus* cases,[232] Guantanamo detainees have also sought relief from the courts using the All Writs Act,[233] principally to prevent their transfer to other countries without notice,[234] but for other reasons too.[235] Use of the All Writs Act by a court is an extraordinary remedy, generally not invoked if there is an alternative remedy available.[236]

Available Remedy

Under Title 28, U.S. code, a court conducting *habeas* review must "award the writ or issue an order directing the respondent to show cause why the writ should not be granted, unless it appears from the application that the detainee is not entitled to it."[237] The court can order either party to expand the record by submitting additional information bearing on the petition.[238] The court may order hearings to assist it in determining the facts, and is authorized to "dispose of the matter as law and justice require,"[239] or in criminal cases, to vacate a sentence, grant a new trial, or order that a prisoner be released.[240]

By contrast, the DTA review procedures do not address the remedies available to detainees who prevail in a challenge. Detainees who succeed in persuading a CSRT that they are not enemy combatants do not have a right to release or even a right initially to be informed of the CSRT's decision. If the CSRT Director approves a finding that a detainee is no longer an enemy combatant, the detainee may be held for as long as it takes the government to arrange for his transfer to his home country or another country willing to provide asylum, during which time he need not be told of the CSRT's conclusion.[241] According to one report of unclassified CSRT records, in the event the CSRT Director disapproves of the finding, new CSRTs may be convened, apparently without notifying or permitting the participation of the detainee, although the government might present new evidence to the new panel.[242]

The Supreme Court viewed the lack of an express power permitting the courts to order the release of a detainee as a factor relevant to the DTA's inadequacy as a substitute proceeding.[243] In the context of CSRT determinations, the government suggested to the Court that remand for new CSRT proceedings would be the appropriate remedy for a determination that an error of law was made or that new evidence must be considered.[244] Whether such a remedy would be acceptable probably depends on whether measures are taken to decrease the risk of error under the CSRT procedures. It seems unlikely that a court would consider itself constitutionally obligated to permit a detainee to enter the United States and be released into the United States unless the detainee has previously formed some ties to the country.[245]

Extraterritorial Scope of Constitutional Writ of Habeas

In *Boumediene*, the Supreme Court held that the constitutional writ of *habeas* extended to persons detained at Guantanamo, even though they are held outside the *de jure* sovereign territory of the United States. Left unresolved in the Court's discussion of the extraterritorial application of the Constitution is the degree to which the writ of *habeas* and other constitutional protections applies to aliens detained in foreign locations other than Guantanamo (e.g., at military facilities in Afghanistan and elsewhere, or at any undisclosed U.S. detention sites overseas). The *Boumediene* Court indicated that it would take a functional approach in resolving such issues, takinginto account "objective factors and practical concerns" in deciding whether the writ extended to aliens detained outside U.S. territory. Practical concerns mentioned in the majority's opinion as relevant to an assessment of the writ's extraterritorial application include the degree and likely duration of U.S. control over the location where the alien is held; the costs of holding the Suspension Clause applicable in a given situation, including the expenditure of funds to permit *habeas* proceedings and the likelihood that the proceedings would compromise or divert attention from a military mission; and the possibility that adjudicating a *habeas* petition would cause friction with the host government.[246] The *Boumediene* Court declined to overrule the Court's prior decision in *Eisentrager*, in which it found that convicted enemy aliens held in post-WWII Germany were precluded from seeking *habeas* relief. Whether enemy aliens are held in a territory that more closely resembles post-WWII Germany than present-day Guantanamo may influence a reviewing court's assessment of whether the writ of *habeas* reaches them, as well as its assessment of the merits of the underlying claims.

Use of Habeas Proceeding to Challenge the Jurisdiction of a Military Commission

Whether detainees who are facing prosecution by a military commission may challenge the jurisdiction of such tribunals prior to the completion of their trial remains unsettled, although the district court has so far declined to enjoin military commissions.[247] Supreme Court precedent suggests that *habeas corpus* proceedings may be invoked to challenge the jurisdiction of a military court even where *habeas corpus* has been suspended.[248] *Habeas* may remain available to defendants who can make a colorable claim not to be enemy combatants within the meaning of the MCA, and therefore to have the right not to be subject to military trial at all, without necessarily having to await a verdict or exhaust the appeals process.[249] Interlocutory challenges contesting whether the charges make out a valid violation of the law of war, for example, seem less likely to be entertained on a *habeas* petition.[250]

Congressional Authority over Federal Courts

Whether Congress can limit the ability of detaineesto bring cases challenging the conditions of their detention may depend on the extent that such challenges are based on constitutional considerations. If it is determined that no other procedure is available to vindicate constitutional rights, then it might bearguedthat the Congress's limitation on the use of *habeas corpus* or other avenues of redress by the detainees is an unconstitutional limitation.

The Constitution contains few requirements regarding the jurisdiction of the federal courts. Article III, Section 1, of the Constitution provides that

> The judicial Power of the United States, shall be vested in one supreme Court, and in such inferior Courts as the Congress may from time to time ordain and establish.[251] The Judges, both of the supreme and inferior Courts, shall hold their Offices during good Behaviour, and shall, at stated Times, receive for their Services, a Compensation, which shall not be diminished during their Continuance in Office.

Although Article III provides for a Supreme Court headed by the Chief Justice of the United States,[252] nothing else about the Court's structure and operation is set forth, leaving the size and composition of the Court, as well as the specifics, if any, of the lower federal courts, to Congress.[253] Utilizing its power to establish inferior courts, Congress has also created the United States district courts,[254] the courts of appeals for the thirteen circuits,[255] and other federal courts.[256]

On its face, there is no limit on the power of Congress to make exceptions to or otherwise regulate the Supreme Court's appellate jurisdiction, to create inferior federal courts, or to specify their jurisdiction. However, the same is true of the Constitution's other grants of legislative authority in Article I and elsewhere, which does not prevent the application of other constitutional principles to those powers. "[T]he Constitution is filled with provisions that grant Congress or the States specific power to legislate in certain areas," Justice Black wrote for the Court in a different context, but "these granted powers are always subject to the limitations that they may not be exercised in a way that violates other specific provisions of the Constitution."[257] Justice Harlan seems to have had the same thought in mind when he said that, with respect to Congress's power over jurisdiction of the federal courts, "what such exceptions and regulations should be it is for Congress, in its wisdom, to establish, having of course due regard to all the Constitution."[258]

Thus, it is clear that while Congress has significant authority over administration of the judicial system, it may not exercise its authority over the courts in a way that violates constitutional rights such as the Fifth Amendment due process clause or precepts of equal protection. For instance, Congress could not limit access to the judicial system based on race or ethnicity.[259] Nor, without amendment of the Constitution, could Congress provide that the courts may take property while denying a right to compensation under the takings clause.[260] In general, the mere fact Congress is exercising its authority over the courts does not serve to insulate such legislation from constitutional scrutiny.

Separation of Powers Issues

It is also clear that Congress may not exercise its authority over the courts in a way that violates precepts of separation of powers. The doctrine of separation of powers is not found in the text of the Constitution, but has been discerned by courts, scholars, and others in the allocation of power in the first three Articles; that is, the "legislative power" is vested in Congress, the "executive power" is vested in the President, and the "judicial power" is vested in the Supreme Court and the inferior federal courts. That interpretation is also consistent with the speeches and writings of the framers. Beginning with *Buckley v. Valeo*,[261] the Supreme Court has reemphasized separation of powers as a vital element in American federal government.[262] Justice Kennedy, in *Boumediene* stressed his view that the writ of *habeas corpus* itself plays an important role in preserving the operation of separation of powers principles.[263]

The federal courts have long held that Congress may not act to denigrate the authority of the judicial branch. In the 1782 decision in *Hayburn's Case*,[264] several Justices objected to a congressional enactment that authorized the federal courts to hear claims for disability pensions for veterans. The courts were to certify their decisions to the Secretary of War, who was authorized either to award each pension or to refuse it if he determined the award was an "imposition or mistaken." The Justices on circuit contended that the law was unconstitutional because the judicial power was committed to a separate department and because the subjecting of a court's opinion to revision or control by an officer of the executive or the legislative branch was not authorized by the Constitution. Congress thereupon repealed the objectionable features of the statute.[265] More recently, the doctrine of separation of powers has been applied to prevent Congress from vesting jurisdiction over common-law bankruptcy claims in non-Article III courts.[266]

Allocation of court jurisdiction by Congress is complicated by the presence of state court systems that can and in some cases do hold concurrent jurisdiction over cases involving questions of federal statutory and constitutional law. Thus, the power of Congress over the federal courts is really the power to determine how federal cases are to be allocated among state courts, federal inferior courts, and the United States Supreme Court. Congress has significant authority to determine which of these various courts will adjudicate such cases, and the method by which this adjudication will occur. For most purposes, the exercise of this power is relatively noncontroversial.

LEGISLATIVE ACTION IN THE 110TH CONGRESS

Congress passed a reporting requirement in the the National Defense Authorization Act for FY2008 addressing detainees at Guantanamo. Several bills have been introduced to authorize and regulate the detention of terrorist suspects, and others would amend the restrictions on detainees' ability to seek *habeas* review. The Senate Judiciary Committee Subcommittee on Terrorism, Technology and Homeland Security held a hearing December 11, 2007, entitled "The Legal Rights of Guantanamo Detainees: What Are They, Should They Be Changed, and Is an End in Sight?"

National Defense Authorization Provisions

The National Defense Authorization Act for Fiscal Year 2008, P.L. 110-181 (H.R. 4986), section 1067 requires the President to submit a report that contains information about detainees at Guantanamo Bay, Cuba, under the control of the Joint Task Force Guantanamo, who are or have ever been classified as "enemy combatants." The report is to identify the number of detainees who are to be tried by military commission; the number of detainees to be released or transferred; the number of detainees to be retained but not charged; and a "description of the actions required to be undertaken, by the Secretary of Defense, possibly the heads of other Federal agencies, and Congress, to ensure that detainees who are subject to an order calling for their release or transfer from the Guantanamo Bay facility have, in fact, been released."

The Senate reported a provision in two earlier versions of the FY2008 Defense authorization bill, S. 1547 and S. 1548, that would have required the Secretary of Defense to convene a CSRT, conducted in accordance with requirements similar to those that apply in military commissions, to determine the status of each detainee who has been held for more than two years as an "unlawful enemy combatant," unless such detainee is undergoing trial or has been convicted by a military commission. The provision adopted the definition of "unlawful enemy combatant" from the MCA, with the addition of an alien who is not a lawful combatant and who has been a "knowing and active participant in an organization that engaged in hostilities against the United States." The provision would have prohibited the use of information acquired through coercion not amounting to cruel, inhuman or degrading treatment (as defined in the DTA) unless the totality of the circumstances renders the statement reliable and possessing sufficient probative value; the interests of justice would best be served by admission of the statement into evidence; and the Tribunal determines that the alleged coercion was incident to the lawful conduct of military operations at the point of apprehension; or the statement was voluntary. The provision was stripped out of the Senate version of the National Defense Authorization Act for Fiscal Year 2008 (H.R. 1585) prior to passage by the Senate.

The House-passed version of the National Defense Authorization Act for Fiscal Year 2009, H.R. 5658, contains a provision that would prevent the Department of Defense from implementing a successor regulation to Army Regulation 190-8, Enemy Prisoners of War, Retained Personnel, Civilian Internees and Other Detainees, until 60 days after Congress is notified,

(§ 1064). The bill would also declare military interrogation to be an inherently governmental function, prohibiting the use of contract personnel to interrogate detainees, (§1077). The Senate is considering a similar provision in its version of the FY2009 National Defense Authorization Act, S. 3001 and S. 3002.

Habeas Corpus Amendments

Several bills have been introduced in both Houses of Congress to amend the *habeas* provisions in the DTA. H.R. 1189, the Habeas Corpus Preservation Act, would provide that the MCA is to be construed to avoid any effect on the right of any U.S. resident to *habeas corpus*. Some of these would also amend the definition of "enemy combatant" in the MCA and revise other aspects of judicial review.

The Military Commissions Habeas Corpus Restoration Act of 2007, H.R. 267, would repeal subsection (e) of 28 U.S.C. § 2241. The bill would add a new Section 1632 to Title 28 providing that no court has jurisdiction to hear cases against the United States or its agents by aliens detained as enemy combatants except for the reviews provided in the DTA and *habeas corpus* petitions. H.R. 2826 would amend 28 U.S.C. § 2241(e) to allow *habeas corpus* actions and requests for injunctive relief against transfer, except in cases of detainees held in an active war zone where the Armed Forces are implementing AR 190-8 or any successor regulation. However, *habeas* challenges related to the decisions of CSRT would be limited to the United States Court of Appeals for the District of Columbia Circuit under the same restrictions in scope that currently apply to appeals of CSRT decisions under the DTA. The bill would also amend 10 U.S.C. § 950j(b) to restore jurisdiction for *habeas corpus*, but not for other actions, related to the prosecution, trial or judgment of a military commission.

H.R. 2710 would repeal 28 U.S.C. § 2241(e) to restore jurisdiction over all cases related to the detention of persons as "enemy combatants," but would prohibit challenges other than *habeas corpus* actions in cases relating to the prosecution, trial, or judgment of a military commission. H.R. 2543, the Military Commissions Revision Act of 2007, would revise the definition of unlawful enemy combatant to cover only a "person who has engaged in, attempted, or conspired to engage in acts of armed hostilities or terrorism against the United States or its co-belligerents, and who is not a lawful enemy combatant." Under the bill, CSRT decisions would no longer be dispositive for purposes of determining the jurisdiction of military commissions. Statements obtained by a degree of coercion less than torture would be admissible in a military commission only if the military judge finds that "the totality of the circumstances indicates that the statement possesses probative value to a reasonable person; the interests of justice would best be served by admitting the statement into evidence; and the interrogation methods used to obtain the statement do not amount to cruel, inhuman or degrading treatment." Habeas corpus jurisdiction would be restored for alien enemy combatants after two years since the date of detention if no criminal charges are pending against the detainee.

S. 185/H.R. 1416, the Habeas Corpus Restoration Act, would repeal subsection (e) of 28 U.S.C. § 2241, but would amend 10 U.S.C. § 950j so that court jurisdiction would continue to be unavailable for detainees seeking to challenge military commissions, except through the limited procedures under the DTA, as amended, and "as otherwise provided in [chapter 47a of title 10, U.S. Code] or in section 2241 of title 28 or any other habeas corpus provision." S. 185 was reported favorably by the Senate Judiciary Committee without amendment.[267] S. 576, the Restoring the Constitution Act of 2007, and its companion bill, H.R. 1415, would amend the definition of "unlawful enemy combatant" in the MCA, 10 U.S.C. § 948a, to mean an individual who is not a lawful combatant who "directly participates in hostilities in a zone of active combat against the United States," or who "planned, authorized, committed, or intentionally aided the terrorist acts on the United States of September 11, 2001" or harbored such a person. A status determination by a CSRT or other tribunal would no longer be dispositive of status under 10 U.S.C. § 948d. The bills would also expressly restrict the definition of "unlawful enemy combatant" for use in designating individuals as eligible for trial by military commission. They would repeal 28 U.S.C. § 2241(e), but limit other causes of action related to the prosecution, trial, and decision of a military commission. DTA provisions related to the limited review of status determinations and final decisions of military commissions would be eliminated, and appeals of military commissions would be routed to the Court of Appeals for the Armed Forces. H.R. 1415 would expand the scope of that review to include questions of fact. With respect to the Geneva Conventions, the bills would eliminate the MCA provision excluding their invocation as a "source of rights" by defendants (10 U.S.C. § 948b(g)), replacing it with a provision that military commission rules determined to be inconsistent with the Geneva Conventions are to have no effect. They would also add a reference to the effect that the President's authority to interpret the Geneva Conventions is subject to congressional oversight and judicial review. Finally, the bills would provide for expedited challenges to the MCA in the D.C. district court. (Provisions amending the War Crimes Act or military commission procedures are not covered in this report.)

S. 1876 would modify the MCA definition of "enemy combatant" to mean persons other than lawful combatants who have engaged in hostilities against the United States or who have purposefully and materially supported hostilities against the United States (other than hostilities engaged in as a lawful enemy combatant). It would also exclude from the definition U.S. citizens and persons admitted for permanent residence in the United States, as well as persons taken into custody in the United States. The bill would provide for jurisdiction in the United States District Court for the District of Columbia to hear *habeas* petitions by persons determined by the United States to have been properly detained as an enemy combatant or persons detained for more than 90 days without such a determination. The court would also have jurisdiction to hear petitions by persons who have been tried by military commissions after they have exhausted the appeals process. Provisions of S. 1876 that address restrictions on detention and liability are described in the next section.

A version of the Habeas Corpus Restoration Act was offered as an amendment to the National Defense Authorization Act, H.R. 1585 (Senate amendment no. 2022), but was not adopted.[268] (After President Bush vetoed H.R. 1585, Congress passed a virtually identical bill, H.R. 4846, which became P.L. 110-181).

H.R. 6247, the "Boumediene Jurisdiction Correction Act," would provide "exclusive original jurisdiction" to hear habeas petitions by persons held under military authority at Guantanamo, apparently including U.S. military personnel, to the "courts established under the Uniform Code of Military Justice and operating in that part of Cuba." Because courts-martial are the only courts under the UCMJ that operate at the naval base, and these are not standing courts that would be capable of accepting such petitions, perhaps the bill should be interpreted to refer the civilian court created by the UCMJ with jurisdiction over Guantanamo. Under this interpretation, all *habeas* petitions by persons detained at Guantanamo would have to be referred to the Court of Appeals for the Armed Forces (CAAF). Otherwise, it seems *habeas* petitions for prisoners at Guantanamo would have to be referred to a commanding officer with court-martial convening authority there, which seems unlikely to provide the sort of independent collateral review that the *Boumediene* Court seemed to view as constitutionally required.

H.R. 6705/S. 3401, the Enemy Combatant Detention Review Act of 2008, would repeal subsection (e) of 28 U.S.C. § 2241. It would grant the U.S.

District Court for the District of Columbia exclusive jurisdiction over, and make it the exclusive venue for consideration of, all *habeas corpus* applications by or on behalf of enemy combatants held at Guantanamo who are not U.S. citizens or aliens who have been admitted for permanent residence in the United States. All such applications would be consolidated before the Chief Judge of the District Court or a designee for consolidated proceedings and determinations on common questions of fact or law. A *habeas corpus* application could be filed to challenge the legality of the continued detention of a covered individual, but not any other claims relating to his detention, transfer, treatment, trial, or conditions of confinement, or any other action against the United States. Applications of persons subject to military commission proceedings would be stayed until those proceedings have been completed. The proposed legislation would also establish procedures for *habeas corpus* review of detainees, including the scope of permitted discovery, protection of national security information, the allowance of video hearings so that a detainee may participate from Guantanamo, and the admission of evidence (including hearsay).

Bills to Regulate Detention

S. 1249 and H.R. 2212 would require the President to close the detention facilities at Guantanamo Bay and either transfer the detainees to the United States for trial (by military proceeding or Article III court) or for detention as enemy combatants asmaybe authorized by Congress; to transfer detainees to an appropriateinternational tribunal operating under U.N. auspices; to transfer detainees to their country of citizenship or a different country for further legal process, where adequate assurances are given that the individual will not be subject to torture or cruel, inhuman, or degrading treatment; or to release them from any further detention.

S. 1876, the "National Security with Justice Act of 2007," would limit extraterritorial detention and rendition, modify the definition of "unlawful enemy combatant"for purposes of military commissions, and extend statutoryhabeascorpus to detainees at Guantanamo. The bill defines "aggrieved person" as an individual who is detained or subjected to rendition overseas by a U.S. officer or agent, except as authorized, excluding any individual who is an international terrorist (a non-U.S. person who "engages in international terrorism or activities in preparation therefor," and any person (apparently including U.S. persons) who knowingly aids, abets or conspires with such a non-U.S. person in the commission of a terrorist act or activity in preparation of a terrorist act). An aggrieved person would have the right to sue the head of the agency or department responsible for his or her unlawful detention or rendition for damages, including punitive damages.

Extraterritorial rendition and detention would generally be permitted only with proper authorization by order of the Foreign Intelligence Surveillance Court (FISC), a court set up to authorize electronic surveillance of agents of foreign powers in the United States. Certain types of renditions and detentions appear to be excluded from these general requirements, including those of persons detained by the United States in Guantanamo on the act's date of enactment who are transferred to a foreign legal jurisdiction, as well as the rendition or detention of individuals detained or transferred by the U.S. Armed Forces under circumstances governed by, and in accordance with, the Geneva Conventions. Otherwise, extraterritorial detention would require the authorization of the President or the Director of National Intelligence based on a certification that the failure to detain that individual "will result in a risk of imminent death or imminent serious bodily injury to any individual or imminent damage to or destruction of any United States facility" or the factual basis exists to demonstrate the individual is an international terrorist and there is reason to believe that the detention or rendition of such person is important to the national security of the United States. An application for detention must be submitted to the FISC within 72 hours in order to detain the person.

H.R. 6705/S. 3401 would expressly authorize the detention of persons who have been engaged in hostilities or who have purposefully and materially supported hostilities against the United States or its co-belligerents on behalf of the Taliban, Al Qaeda, or associated forces. It would bar a court from releasing a person into the United States who has been designated as an "enemy combatant" by a CSRT (other thanaU.S. citizenor an alien admitted into the U.S. for permanent residence)and also make such a person ineligible for a entry visa or any immigration status, subject to the waiver of the President. If a court were to grant a detainee's *habeas* application and order his release, he would be placed in the custody of the Secretary of Homeland Security for transfer to the detainee's country of citizenship or a third country.

CONCLUSION

The Administration's policy of detaining wartime captives and suspected terrorists at the Guantanamo Bay Naval Station has raised a host of novel legal questions regarding, among other matters, the relative powers of the President and Congress to fight terrorism, as well as the power of the courts to review the actions of the political branches. The DTA was Congress's first effort to impose limits on the President's conduct of the Global War on Terrorism and to prescribe a limited role for the courts. The Supreme Court's decision striking the DTA provision that attempted to eliminate the courts' *habeas* jurisdiction may be seen as an indication that the Court will continue to play a role in determining the ultimate fate of the detainees at Guantanamo. However, the Court did not foreclose all options available to Congress to streamline *habeas* proceedings involving detainees at Guantanamo or elsewhere in connection with terrorism. Instead, it indicated that the permissibility of such measures will be weighed in the context of relevant circumstances and exigencies.

As a general matter, the courts have not accepted the view that the President has inherent constitutional authority to detain those he suspects may be involved in international terrorism. Rather, the courts have looked to the language of the AUMF and other legislation to determine the contours of presidential power. The Supreme Court has interpreted the AUMF with the assumption that Congress intended for the President to pursue the conflict in accordance with traditional law-of-war principles, and has upheld the detention of a "narrow category" of persons who fit the traditional definition of "enemy combatant" under the law of war. Other courts have been willing to accept a broader definition of "enemy combatant" to permit the detention of individuals who were not captured in circumstances suggesting their direct participation in hostilities against the United States, but a plurality of the Supreme Court warned that a novel interpretation of the scope of the law of war might cause their understanding of permissible executive action to unravel. Consequently, Congress may be called upon to consider legislation to support the full range of authority asserted by the executive branch in connection with the GWOT. In the event the Court finds that the detentions in question are fully supported by statutory authorization, whether on the basis of existing law or new enactments, the key issue is likely to be whether the detentions comport with due process of law under the Constitution.

End Notes

[1] 542 U.S. 507 (2004).
[2] 542 U.S. 466 (2004).
[3] Hamdan v. Rumsfeld, 464 F. Supp. 2d 9 (D.D.C. 2006).
[4] Boumediene v. Bush, 476 F.3d 981 (D.C. Cir. 2007).
[5] Boumediene v. Bush, 127 S.Ct. 1478 (2007).
[6] Boumediene v. Bush, 127 S.Ct. 3078 (2007).
[7] Boumediene v. Bush, 553 U.S. __, 128 S.Ct. 2229 (2008).
[8] *Id.*, 128 S.Ct. at 2270, 2275.
[9] Al-Marri v. Wright, 487 F.3d 160 (4th Cir. 2007).
[10] Al-Marri v. Pucciarrelli, Case No. 06-7427 (4th Cir.).
[11] Al-Marri v. Pucciarrelli, __ F.3d __, 2008 WL 2736787 (4th Cir. 2008).
[12] The two most relevant conventions are the Geneva Convention Relative to the Treatment of Prisoners of War, August 12, 1949, 6 U.S.T. 3317 (hereinafter "GPW"); and the Geneva Convention Relative to the Protection of Civilian Persons in Time of War, August 12, 1949, 6 U.S.T. 3516 (hereinafter "GC").
[13] White House Memorandum, "Humane Treatment of al Qaeda and Taliban Detainees" (February 7, 2002), *available at* [http://www.washingtonpost.com/wp-srv/nation/documents/ 020702bush.pdf].
[14] For more history and analysis, see CRS Report RL31367, ***Treatment of 'Battlefield Detainees'*** *in the War on Terrorism*, by Jennifer K. Elsea.
[15] Order on Detention, Treatment, and Trial of Certain Non-Citizens in the War against Terrorism, November 13, 2001, 66 *Federal Register* 57833 (2001)(hereinafter "MO" or "military order").
[16] For an analysis of the military commission rules, see CRS Report RL33688, *The Military Commissions Act of 2006: Analysis of Procedural Rules and Comparison with Previous DOD Rules and the Uniform Code of Military Justice*, by Jennifer K. Elsea.
[17] 10 U.S.C. § 801 *et seq.*
[18] 542 U.S. 466 (2004).
[19] 339 U.S. 763 (1950).
[20] *Rasul*, 542 U.S. at 478-79. When *Eisentrager* was decided in 1950, the *Rasul* majority found, the "respective jurisdictions" of federal district courts were understood to extend no farther than the geographical boundaries of the districts (citing Ahrens v. Clark, 335 U.S. 188 (1948)). According to the Court, that understanding was altered by a line of cases, recognized in Braden v. 30th Judicial Circuit Court of Ky., 410 U.S. 484 (1973), as overruling the statutory interpretation that hadestablished the "inflexible jurisdictional rule" upon which *Eisentrager* was implicitly based. Justice Scalia, with Chief Justice Rehnquist and Justice Thomas, dissented, arguing that the *habeas* statute on its face requires a federal district court with territorial jurisdiction over the detainee. The dissenters would have read *Braden* as distinguishing *Ahrens* rather than overruling it. For more analysis of the *Rasul* opinion, see CRS Report RS21884, *The Supreme Court 2003 Term: Summary and Analysis of Opinions Related to Detainees in the War on Terrorism*, by Jennifer K. Elsea.
[21] *Rasul*, 542 U.S. at 475 (citing *Eisentrager*, 339 U.S. at 777).
[22] 28 U.S.C. § 1331("The district courts shall have original jurisdiction of all civil actions arising under the Constitution, laws, or treaties of the United States.").
[23] 28 U.S.C. § 1350 ("The district courts shall have original jurisdiction of any civil action by an alien for a tort only, committed in violation of the law of nations or a treaty of the United States.").
[24] *Rasul*, 542 U.S. at 484 ("nothing in *Eisentrager* or in any of our other cases categorically excludes aliens detained in military custody outside the United States from the 'privilege of litigation' in U.S. courts").

[25] The Court noted that "*Eisentrager* made quite clear that all six of the facts critical to its disposition were relevant only to the question of the prisoners' *constitutional* entitlement to habeas corpus." *Rasul*, 542 U.S. at 476 (emphasis original).

[26] Hamdan v. Rumsfeld, 126 S.Ct. 2749, 2793 (2006)(characterizing the *Eisentrager* decision, 339 U.S. 763, 790(1950), as having rejected the treaty claim "on the merits"). Justice Kennedy's *Boumediene* opinion rejected the view that *Eisentrager* imposed a strict jurisdictional test based solely on the sovereignty of the territory involved, finding instead that all of the "practical considerations" considered in the opinion were integral to the ultimate holding. *Boumediene* at 2257.

[27] *See* Department of Defense (DOD) Fact Sheet, "Combatant Status Review Tribunals," *available at* [http://www.defenselink.mil/news/Jul2004/d20040707factsheet.pdf]. CSRT proceedings are modeled on the procedures of Army Regulation (AR) 190-8, Enemy Prisoners of War, Retained Personnel, Civilian Internees and Other Detainees (1997), which establishes administrative procedures to determine the status of detainees under the Geneva Conventions and prescribes their treatment in accordance with international law. It does not include a category for "unlawful" or "enemy" combatants, who would presumably be covered by the other categories.

[28] *See* DOD Press Release, "Combatant Status Review Tribunal Order Issued" (June 7, 2004), *available at* [http://www.defenselink.mil/releases/2004/nr20040707-0992.html]; Memorandum from the Deputy Secretary of Defense to the Secretary of the Navy, Order Establishing Combatant Status Review Tribunal, July 7, 2004 (hereinafter "CSRT Order"), *available at* [http://www.defenselink.mil/news/Jul2004/d20040707review.pdf]; Memorandum from Deputy Secretary of Defense, Implementation of Combatant Status Review Tribunals Procedures for Enemy Combatants Detained at U.S. Naval Base Guantanamo Bay, Cuba, July 14, 2006 (hereinafter "CSRT Implementing Directive"), *available at* [http://www.defenselink.mil/news/Aug2006/d20060809CSRTProcedures.pdf].

[29] *See* Josh White and Shailagh Murray, *Guantanamo Ruling Renews The Debate Over Detainees*, WASH. POST, June 6, 2007, at A3.

[30] United States v. Khadr, No. 07-001, (U.S.C.M.C.R. September 7, 2007) (finding CSRT designation alone insufficient to confer jurisdiction on military commission, but holding that the military commission judge has the inherent authority to determine the status of the accused).

[31] Witnesses from within the U.S. Armed Forces are not "reasonably available" if their participation, as determined by their commanders, would adversely affect combat or support operations. CSRT Implementing Directive, *supra* note 28, at encl. 1, para. G(9)(a). All other witnesses, apparently including those from other agencies, are not "reasonably available" if they decline to attend or cannot be reached, or if security considerations prevents their presence. *Id.* at encl. 1, para. G(9)(b). It is unclear who makes the security determination. Non-government witnesses appear at their own expense. Testimony is under oath and may be provided in writing or by telephone or video.

[32] CSRT Order, *supra* note 28, at 1.

[33] CSRT Implementing Directive, *supra* note 28, at encl. 1, para. B.

[34] *Id.* at encl. 1, para. F.

[35] *Id* at encl. 1, para. C(2). In an affidavit submitted in DTA litigation, the government acknowledged that it has not utilized the procedures set forth in the CSRT Implementing Directive. *See* Bismullah v. Gates, 501 F.3d 178, 194-95 (D.C. Cir. 2007) (order on motions) (Rogers, J. Concurring) (citing differences between written procedures and those described by Rear Admiral James M. McGarrah in the *Boumediene* case). Rather than having a JAG officer in the rank of O-3 or above compile government information, the Department of Defense has utilized research, collection, and coordination teams to gather information to be assessed by a "case writer" who has "received approximately two weeks of training." *Id.* at 94. Thus, the reporter assigned to represent the government's case may not have had access to all government information.

[36] CSRT Implementing Directive, *supra* note 28, at encl. 1, para. G(7) & (11).
[37] *Id.* at encl. 1, para. G(8).
[38] *Id.* at encl. 10.
[39] *Id.* at encl. 1, para. E(3)(a).
[40] *Id.* at encl. 1, para. H(7).
[41] *Id.* at encl. 2, para. D (the personal representative is required to explain to the represented detainee that he or she is neither the attorney or advocate for the detainee, and that any information provided by the detainee is not confidential).
[42] *Id.* at encl. 1, para. I(9)-(10).
[43] *See* DOD Press Release, "DoD Announces Draft Detainee Review Policy" (March 3, 2004), *available at* [http://www.defenselink.mil/releases/2004/nr20040303-0403.html]; Memorandum from Deputy Secretary of Defense, Revised Implementation of Administrative Review Procedures for Enemy Combatants Detained at U.S. Navy Base, Guantanamo Bay, Cuba (July 14, 2006), *available at* [http://www.defenselink.mil/news/Aug2006/d20060809ARBProceduresMemo.pdf].
[44] CSRT Implementing Directive, *supra* note 28, at encl. 10 (implementing Detainee Treatment Act provisions).
[45] 339 U.S. 763 (1950) (holding that the federal courts did not have jurisdiction to hear a petition on behalf of German citizens who had been convicted byU.S. military commissions in China because the writ of *habeas corpus* was not available to "enemy alien[s], who at no relevant time and in no stage of [their] captivity [have] been within [the court's] jurisdiction").
[46] Khalid v. Bush, 355 F. Supp. 2d 311 (D.D.C. 2005); Hamdan v. Rumsfed, 464 F. Supp.2d 9 (D.D.C. 2006).
[47] Al Odah v. United States, 346 F. Supp. 2d 1 (D.D.C. 2004).
[48] Hamdan v. Rumsfeld, 344 F. Supp. 2d 152 (D.D.C. 2004), *rev'd* 415 F.3d 33 (D.C. Cir.), *rev'd* 548 U.S. 557 (2006).
[49] Boumediene v. Bush, 476 F.3d 981 (D.C. Cir. 2007).
[50] Al-Marri v. Gates, Case No. 05-2259 (D.S.C. filed March 13, 2008).
[51] 355 F. Supp. 2d 311 (D.D.C. 2005), *vacated and dismissed sub nom.* Boumediene v. Bush, 476 F.3d 981 (D.C. Cir. 2007), *rev'd* Boumediene v. Bush, 553 U.S. __, 128 S.Ct. 2229 (2008).
[52] Authorization for Use of Military Force ("the AUMF"), P.L. 107-40, 115 Stat. 224 (2001).
[53] Although the MO authorized detention as well as trial by military commissions, only fifteen of the detainees were formally designated as subject to the MO.
[54] 355 F. Supp. 2d at 314.
[55] *Id.* at 320.
[56] *Id.* at 318. Judge Leon wrote:

> The President's ability to make the decisions necessary to effectively prosecute a Congressionally authorized armed conflict must be interpreted expansively. Indeed, the Constitution does not delegate to Congress the power to "conduct" or to "make" war; rather, Congress has been given the power to "declare" war. This critical distinction lends considerable support to the President's authority to make the operational and tactical decisions necessary during an ongoing conflict. Moreover, there can be no doubt that the President's power to act at a time of armed conflict is at its strongest when Congress has specifically authorized the President to act.

[57] *Id.* at 326.
[58] *Id.* at 327. It may be argued that the *habeas* statute itself (28 U.S.C. § 2241), which authorizes challenges of detention based on treaty violations, provided a means for private enforcement, at least prior to its amendment by the MCA. *See Eisentrager*, 339 U.S. at 789 (while noting that the 1929 Geneva Convention did not provide for private enforcement, considering but rejecting the *habeas* claim that the treaty vitiated jurisdiction of military commission).

[59] *Id.* at 330 (citations omitted).

[60] 355 F. Supp. 2d 443 (D.D.C. 2005), *vacated and dismissed sub nom.* Boumediene v. Bush, 476 F.3d 981 (D.C. Cir. 2007), ***rev'd*** Boumediene v. Bush, 553 U.S. __, 128 S.Ct. 2229 (2008).

[61] *Id.* at 465 (citing *Hamdi v. Rumsfeld*).

[62] *Id.* at 475 (internal citations omitted).

[63] *Id.* at 476.

[64] 344 F. Supp. 2d 152 (D.D.C. 2004), 415 F.3d 33 (D.C. Cir. 2005), ***rev'd*** 548 U.S. 557 (2006).

[65] 10 U.S.C. §§ 801 *et seq.*

[66] There are four Conventions, the most relevant of which is The Geneva Convention Relative to the Treatment of Prisoners of War, August 12, 1949, 6 U.S.T. 3317 (hereinafter "GPW").

[67] 344 F. Supp. 2d at 161.

[68] GPW art. 3. For a discussion of Common Article 3, see CRS Report RL31367, *Treatment of "Battlefield Detainees" in the War on Terrorism*, by Jennifer K. Elsea.

[69] P.L. 109-148, §1005(e)(1) provides that "no court ... shall have jurisdiction to hear or consider ... an application for ... habeas corpus filed by ... an alien detained ... at Guantanamo Bay." The provision was not yet law when the appellate court decided against the petitioner, Hamdan v. Rumsfeld, 415 F.3d 33 (D.C. Cir. 2005), ***rev'd*** 548 U.S. 557 (2006). At issue was whether this provision applies to pending cases. The Court found that the provision did not apply to Hamdan's petition, because the case did not fall under either of the categories of cases over which the DTA had created appellate review in the D.C. Circuit. The Court did not resolve whether the DTA affects cases that fall under the DTA's provisions regarding final review of Combatant Status Review Tribunals, for which *habeas* review was eliminated as to pending cases. *Hamdan*, 126 S.Ct. at 2769, and n.14.

[70] *Id.* at 2763-64. To resolve the question, the majority employed canons of statutory interpretation supplemented by legislative history, avoiding the question of whether the withdrawal of the Court's jurisdiction would constitute a suspension of the Writ of Habeas Corpus, or whether it would amount to impermissible "court-stripping." Justice Scalia, joined by Justices Alito and Thomas in his dissent, interpreted the DTA as a revocation of jurisdiction.

[71] *Id.* at 2769-70. The court below had also rejected this argument, 413 F.3d 33, 36 (D.C. Cir. 2005).

[72] *See Hamdan*, 126 S.Ct. at 2771 (stating that the bodies established by the Department of Defense to review the decisions of military commissions "clearly lack the structural insulation from military influence that characterizes the Court of Appeals for the Armed Forces....").

[73] 10 U.S.C. § 821 ("The provisions of [the UCMJ] conferring jurisdiction upon courts-martial do not deprive military commissions, provost courts, or other military tribunals of concurrent jurisdiction with respect to offenders or offenses that by statute or by the law of war may be tried by military commissions, provost courts, or other military tribunals.")

[74] *Hamdan*, 126 S.Ct. at 2773 (citing Congress's powers to "declare War ... and make Rules concerning Captures on Land and Water," Art. I, §8, cl. 11, to "raise and support Armies," *Id.*, cl. 12, to "define and punish ... Offences against the Law of Nations," *Id.*, cl. 10, and "To make Rules for the Government and Regulation of the land and naval Forces," *Id.*, cl. 14.).

[75] P.L. 107-40, 115 Stat. 224 (2001).

[76] *Hamdan*, 126 S.Ct. at 2775.

[77] 28 U.S.C. § 2241(c)(3)(permitting petitions by prisoners "in custody in violation of the Constitution or laws or treaties of the United States").

[78] *See* 415 F.3d at 39 (citing Johnson v. Eisentrager, 339 U.S. 763, 789, n. 14(1950)).

[79] *Hamdan*, 126 S.Ct. at 2794.

[80] GPW art. 3 § 1(d). The identical provision is included in each of the four Geneva Conventions and applies to any "conflict not of an international character." The majority declined to accept the President's interpretation of Common Article 3 as inapplicable to the conflict

with al Qaeda and interpreted the phrase "in contradistinction to a conflict between nations," which the Geneva Conventions designate a "conflict of international character". *Hamdan*, 126 S.Ct. at 2795.

[81] *Id.* at 2796-97 (plurality opinion); *Id.* (Kennedy, J., concurring) at 2804. Justice Stevens, joined by Justices Ginsburg, Breyer, and Souter, further based their conclusion on the basis that M.C.O. No. 1 did not meet all criteria of art. 75 of Protocol I to the Geneva Conventions of 1949, adopted in 1977 (Protocol I). While the United States is not party to Protocol I, the plurality noted that many authorities regard it as customary international law.

[82] 542 U.S. 466 (2004).

[83] 542 U.S. 507, 535 (2004).

[84] *See, e.g., Oversight of the Department of Justice: Hearing Before the Senate Judiciary Committee*, 107th Cong. (2002) (testimony of Attorney General John Ashcroft) (arguing that a statute that could be read to interfere withthe executive power to detain enemy combatants must be interpreted otherwise to withstand constitutional scrutiny).

[85] Youngstown Sheet & Tube Co. v. Sawyer, 343 U.S. 579 (1952).

[86] For information about relevant legislation, see CRS Report RL31600, *The Department of Defense Rules for Military Commissions: Analysis of Procedural Rules and Comparison with Proposed Legislation and the Uniform Code of Military Justice*.

[87] Al-Marri v. Rumsfeld, 360 F.3d 707 (7th Cir. 2004), *cert. denied* 543 U.S. 809 (2004).

[88] Al-Marri v. Hanft, 378 F. Supp.2d 673 (D. S.C. 2005) (order denying summary judgment).

[89] Al-Marri v. Pucciarelli, slip op. at 4 (4th Cir. 2008)(Motz, J., concurring)(citingdeclaration Jeffrey N. Rapp, Director of the Joint Intelligence Task Force for Combating Terrorism).

[90] Al-Marri v. Wright, 443 F. Supp. 2d 774 (D. S.C. 2006) (citing Hamdi v. Rumsfeld, 542 U.S. 507 (2004)). With respect to the "due process hearing" required to establish that an

> enemy combatant is properly held, the *Hamdi* plurality stated that: enemy combatant proceedings may be tailored to alleviate their uncommon potential to burden the Executive at a time of ongoing military conflict. Hearsay, for example, may need to be accepted as the most reliable available evidence fromthe Government in such a proceeding. Likewise, the Constitution would not be offended by a presumption in favor of the Government's evidence, so long as that presumption remained a rebuttable one and fair opportunity for rebuttal were provided. Thus, once the Government puts forth credible evidence that the habeas petitioner meets the enemy-combatant criteria, the onus could shift to the petitioner to rebut that evidence with more persuasive evidence that he falls outside the criteria.

443 F. Supp. 2d 778 (quoting *Hamdi* at 534).

[91] *Id.* at 778-80.

[92] The court held that the MCA requires a two-step process for determining whether persons are properly detained as enemy combatants, but that the President's determination of the petitioner's "enemy combatant" status fulfilled onlythe first step. The court next found that Al-Marri could not be said to be awaiting such a determination within the meaning of the MCA, inasmuch as the government was arguing on the merits that the presidential determination had provided all of the process that was due, and the government had offered the possibility of bringing Al-Marri before a CSRT only as an alternative course of action in the event the petition were dismissed. Further, the majority looked to the legislative history of the MCA, from which it divined that Congress did not intend to replace *habeas* review with the truncated review available under the amended DTA in the case of aliens within the United States, who it understood to have a constitutional as opposed to merely statutory entitlement to seek habeas review. Al-Marri v. Wright , 487 F.3d 160, 172 (4th Cir. 2007), *vacated sub nom.* Al-Marri v. Pucciarelli, __F.3d __ (2008)(per curiam).

[93] *Id.* at 196.

[94] 423 F.3d 386 (4th Cir. 2005). The government is no longer holding Jose Padilla as an enemy combatant, having turned him over to civil authorities for trial on charges associatedwith terrorism.
[95] *Al-Marri*, 487 F.3d at 180 (citing *Hamdi* at 516-17)(emphasis in original).
[96] *Id.* (citing *Padilla*, 423 F.3d at 390-91).
[97] 317 U.S. 1 (1942).
[98] *Al-Marri*, 487 F.3d at 179 (citing *Quirin*, 317 U.S. at 37-38; *Hamdi*, 542 U.S. at 519; *Padilla*, 423 F.3d at 391).
[99] 71 U.S. (4 Wall.) 2 (1866).
[100] *Al-Marri* at 189.
[101] *Id.* at 196 (Hudson, J., dissenting).
[102] Al-Marri v. Pucciarelli, __F.3d __, 2008 WL 2736787 (4th Cir. 2008)(per curiam). The intervening Supreme Court decision in *Boumediene* led the court to reject the government's contention that the MCA had divested the court of jurisdiction.
[103] *Id.* at *13 (Motz, J. concurring)(citing *Hamdi*, 542 U.S. at 518). Judge Motz, joined by three other judges, characterized leading precedents as sharing two characteristics:

> (1) they look to law-of-war principles to determine who fits within the "legal category" of enemy combatant; and (2) following the law of war, they rest enemy combatant status on affiliation with the military arm of an enemy nation.

Under their interpretation of the law of war, there is no combatant status in non-international armed conflict, where detention is controlled by domestic law. For a discussion of U.S. practice with respect to the wartime detention of suspected enemies, whether civilians or combatants, see CRS Report RL31724, *Detention of American Citizens as Enemy Combatants*, by Jennifer K. Elsea.
[104] *Al-Marri*, at *32.
[105] *Id.* at *32 (Traxler, J., concurring).
[106] *Id.* at *37. Judge Traxler further suggested that the types of activities that would distinguish a combatant from a civilian enemy would include violent activities. *See id.* At *39 (describing the allegations that al-Marri "directly allied himself with al Qaeda abroad, volunteered for assignments (including a martyr mission), received training and funding from al Qaeda abroad, was dispatched by al Qaeda to the United States as an al Qaeda operative with orders to serve as a sleeper agent, and was tasked with facilitating and ultimately committing terrorist attacks against the United States within this country"). The dissenting judges suggested similar definitions for determining who may be treated as an "enemy combatant." *See id.* at *61 (Williams, J., concurring in part and dissenting in part)(defining enemy combatant covered by the AUMF as "an individual who meets two criteria: (1) he attempts or engages in belligerent acts against the United States, either domestically or in a foreign combat zone; (2) on behalf of an enemy force"); *id.* at *99 (Wilkinson, J., concurring in part and dissenting in part)(proposing two-part test in which "an 'enemy' is any individual who is (1) a member of (2) an organization or nation against whom Congress has declared war or authorized the use of military force" and a combatant is " a person who knowingly plans or engages in conduct that harms or aims to harm persons or property for the purpose of furthering the military goals of an enemy nation or organization").
[107] *See id.* at *53 (Gregory, J., concurring).
[108] *Id.* at *47. Judge Traxler formulated a general rule under which such enemy combatants "would be entitled to the normal due process protections available to all within this country, including an opportunity to confront and question witnesses against him[, unless] the government can demonstrate to the satisfaction of the district court that this is impractical, outweighed by national security interests, or otherwise unduly burdensome because of the nature of the capture and the potential burdens imposed on the government to produce non-hearsay evidence and accede to discovery requests, [in which case] alternatives should be considered and employed." *Id.* at *49.

[109] Section 1002 of P.L. 109-148 requires DOD to follow the Army Field Manual for intelligence interrogation. *See* DEPARTMENT OF THE ARMY FIELD MANUAL 34-52, INTELLIGENCE INTERROGATION (1992), *available at* [http://www4.army.mil/ocpa/reports/ArmyIGDetaineeAbuse/FM34-52IntelInterrogation.pdf] (September 1, 2004). For an analysis of the approved interrogation procedures, see CRS Report RL32567, *Lawfulness of Interrogation Techniques under the Geneva Conventions*, by Jennifer K. Elsea.

[110] Section 1003 of P.L. 109-148. *See* CRS Report RL33655, *Interrogation of Detainees: Overview of the McCain Amendment*, by Michael John Garcia.

[111] Section 1003(d) of P.L. 109-148. For more information, see CRS Report RL32438, *U.N. Convention Against Torture (CAT): Overview and Application to Interrogation Techniques*, by Michael John Garcia.

[112] Section 1005 of P.L. 109-148 (denying aliens in military custody privilege to file writ of *habeas corpus* or "any other action against the United States or its agents relating to any aspect of the[ir] detention. . .").

[113] Section 1004 of P.L. 109-148 provides a defense in litigation related to "specific operational practices," involving detention and interrogation where the defendant

> did not know that the practices were unlawful and a person of ordinarysense and understanding would not know the practices were unlawful. Good faith reliance on advice of counsel should be an important factor, among others, to consider in assessing whether a person of ordinary sense and understanding would have known the practices to be unlawful.

[114] *See* Eric Schmitt, *Exception Sought in Detainee Abuse Ban*, N.Y. TIMES, October 25, 2005, at 16.

[115] 151 CONG. REC. S12667 (daily ed. November 10, 2005)(introduced by Sen. Graham, passed by roll call vote, 49 - 42), as amended by S.Amdt. 2524, 151 CONG. REC. S12771 (daily ed. November 14, 2005).

[116] The amendment refers to both the Combatant Status Review Tribunals ("CSRTs"), the initial administrative procedure to confirm the detainees' status as enemy combatants, and the Administrative Review Boards, which were established to provide annual review that the detainees' continued detention is warranted.

[117] Boumediene v. Bush, 553 U.S. __, 128 S.Ct. 2229, 2275 (2008).

[118] Senator Frist introduced the Administration's proposal as the "Bringing Terrorists to Justice Act of 2006," S. 3861. The Senate Armed Services Committee reported favorably a bill called the "Military Commissions Act of 2006" (S. 3901), which was in many respects similar to the Administration's proposal, but varied with respect to jurisdiction and some rules of evidence. The House Armed Services Committee approved H.R. 6054, also called the "Military Commissions Act of 2006," which closely tracked the Administration's proposal. After reaching an agreement with the White House with respect to several provisions in S. 3901, Senator McCain introduced S. 3930, again entitled the "Military Commissions Act of 2006." Representative Hunter subsequently introduced a modified version of H.R. 6054 as H.R. 6166, which the House of Representatives passed on September 28, 2006. A manager's amendment to S. 3930, substantially identical to the bill passed by the House, was passed by the Senate the following day.

[119] P.L. 109-366. For a further description of the procedures associated with these military commissions, see CRS Report RL33688, *The Military Commissions Act of 2006: Analysis of Procedural Rules and Comparison with Previous DOD Rules and the Uniform Code of Military Justice*, by Jennifer K. Elsea.

[120] MCA § 5.

[121] 10 U.S.C. § 950g(b).

[122] MCA § 7.

[123] 28 U.S.C. § 2241.

[124] GPW art. 3 § 1(d). *See Hamdan*, 126 S.Ct. at 2796-2797 (noting the application of this provision of the Geneva Conventions to detainees through the UCMJ Article 21).

[125] MCA § 5(a) provides that "No person may invoke the Geneva Conventions or any protocols thereto in any habeas corpus or other civil action or proceeding to which the United States, or a current or former officer, employee, member of the Armed Forces, or other agent of the United States is a party as a source of rights in any court of the United States or its States or territories."

[126] MCA § 3 (10 U.S.C. § 948c) provides that "No alien unlawful enemy combatant subject to trial by military commission under this chapter may invoke the Geneva Conventions as a source of rights."

[127] MCA § 3 (10 U.S.C. § 948b(f), as amended) provides that a military commission is a "regularly constituted court, affording all the necessary 'judicial guarantees which are recognized as indispensable by civilized peoples' for purposes of common Article 3 of the Geneva Conventions." While this language could be construed as directing a court to find that the MCA does not conflict with the Geneva Conventions, a better reading would appear to be that, to the extent that there is a conflict between the MCA and the Geneva Conventions, that the MCA should be given precedence. *See generally* Robertson v. Seattle Audubon Soc'y, 503 U.S. 429 (1992).

[128] MCA § 6(a)(3)(A) provides that "the President has the authority for the United States to interpret the meaning and application of the Geneva Conventions and to promulgate higher standards and administrative regulations for violations of treaty obligations which are notgrave breaches of the Geneva Conventions."

[129] *See, e.g.*, id. (President is given power to promulgate higher standards and administrative regulations for violations of treaty obligations).

[130] *See, e.g.*, MCA § 6(a)(3)(B)("No foreign or international source of law shall supply a basis for a rule of decision in the courts of the United States in interpreting the prohibitions enumerated in subsection (d) of such section 2441.").

[131] *See* Dickerson v. United States, 530 U.S. 428, 438 (2000)(striking down congressional statute purporting to overturn the Court's Fourth Amendment rulingin *Miranda v. Arizona);* City of Boerne v. Flores, 521 U.S. 507, 519 (1997)(Congress' enforcement power under the Fourteenth Amendment does not extend to the power to alter the Constitution); Plaut v. Spendthrift Farm, 514 U.S. 211, 225 (Congress may not disturb final court rulings).

[132] 80 U.S. (13 Wall.) 128 (1871).

[133] The Court struck down the law, essentially holding that the Congress had an illegitimate purpose in passage of the law. "[T]he language of the proviso shows plainly that it does not intend to withhold appellate jurisdiction except as a means to an end. Its great and controllingpurpose is to deny to pardons granted by the President the effect which this court had adjudged them to have. . . . It seems to us that this is not an exercise of the acknowledged power of Congress to make exceptions and prescribe regulations to the appellate power." 80 U.S. at 146. The Court also found that the statue impaired the effect of presidential pardon, and thus "infringe[ed] the constitutional power of the Executive." *Id.* at 147.

[134] *See generally* Miller v. French, 530 U.S. 327, 350-51 (2000)(Souter, J., concurring).

[135] MCA § 6(a)(3)(B).

[136] "If the country with which the treaty is made is dissatisfied with the action of the legislative department, it may present its complaint to the executive head of the government, and take such other measures as it may deem essential for the protection of its interests. Thecourts can afford no redress. Whether the complaining nation has just cause of complaint,or our country was justified in its legislation, are not matters for judicial cognizance."Whitney v. Robertson 124 U.S. 190, 194 (1888).

[137] MCA § 5(a). It is unclear why the MCA addresses the application of the Geneva Convention to *habeas corpus* proceeding brought by detainees, since such suits are precluded by the DTA and the MCA. Section 1405(e) of P.L. 109-63; MCA, §7(a). It may be intended to

apply to *habeas* cases brought by U.S. citizens or by aliens who do not fall under the definition of "enemy combatant." On the other hand, as will be discussed *infra*, there may be constitutional issues associated with limiting access of enemy combatants to *habeas corpus* proceeding. In the event the *habeas* restrictions of the DTA are found to be unconstitutional, then this provision may become relevant to those proceedings.

138 Executive Order 13340, *Interpretation of the Geneva Conventions Common Article 3 as Applied to a Program of Detention and Interrogation Operated by the Central Intelligence Agency*, 72 Fed. Reg. 40707 (July 20, 2007).

139 *See* Karen DeYoung, *Court Told It Lacks Power in Detainee Cases*, WASH. POST, October 20, 2006, at A18 (reporting notice submitted by Justice Department to courts of intention to move for dismissal of pending enemy combatant cases).

140 Al-Marri v. Wright, 487 F.3d 160 (4th Cir. 2007), *vacated sub nom.* Al-Marri v. Pucciarelli, __F.3d __ (2008)(per curiam).

141 *See* S. 4081 and H.R. 6381, 109th Cong.

142 *See, e.g.*, Scott Shane and Adam Liptak, *Detainee Bill Shifts Power to President*, N.Y. TIMES, September 30, 2006, at A1.

143 542 U.S. 507 (2004).

144 P.L. 107-40, 115 Stat. 224 (2001).

145 542 U.S. at 516.

146 Padilla v. Hanft, 423 F.3d 386 (4th Cir. 2005).

147 Bismullah v. Gates, 501 F.3d 178 (*Bismullah I*), ***reh'g denied*** 503 F.3d 137(D.C. Cir. 2007) (*Bismullah II*).

148 *Bismullah II*, 503 F. 3d 137 (D.C. Cir. 2007).

149 Bismullah v. Gates, 514 F.3d 1291 (D.C. Cir. 2008).

150 Gates v. Bismullah (U.S., filed February 14, 2008) (07-1054).

151 Gates v. Bismullah, 128 S.Ct. 2960 (2008).

152 Bismullah v. Gates, Case No. 06-1197, Order (D.C. Cir. August 22, 2008) (*per curium*), available at [http://www.scotusblog.com/wp/wp-content/uploads/2008/08/bismullah-order8-22-08.pdf].

153 *See Bismullah I*, 501 F.3d at 193 (Rogers, J. Concurring).

154 *Id.*

155 *Id.* (citing differences between written procedures and those described by Rear Admiral James M. McGarrah in the *Boumediene* case).

156 Parhat v. Gates, — - F.3d——, 2008 WL 2576977, No. 06-1397 (June 20, 2008).

157 Although Parhat argued that the DOD's regulatory definition of "enemy combatant" exceeded the scope authorized by the 2001 AUMF, the Circuit Court declined to reach this issue, finding that the government provided insufficient evidence to demonstrate that Parhat met the DOD's own regulatory definition.

158 *Id.*, 2008 WL 2576977 at *7, quoting Dept. of Def. Order Establishing Combatant Status Review Tribunal (July 7, 2004), at 1.

159 *Id.*

160 *Id.*, 2008 WL 2576977 at *11.

161 *Id.*

162 *Id.*, 2008 WL 2576977 at *14.

163 *Parhat*, 2008 WL 2576977 at *14.

164 *Id.*, 2008 WL 2576977 at *15.

165 Husaifa Parhat's Motion for Immediate Release on Parole into the Continental United States Pending Final Judgment on His Habeas Petition, In re: Guantanamo Bay Litigation, No. 05-1509 (July 23, 2008).

166 For further discussion, see CRS Report RL34536, *Boumediene v. Bush: Guantanamo Detainees' Right to Habeas Corpus*, by Michael John Garcia.

167 The practice of divesting courts of jurisdiction over particular issues is sometimes referred to as "court-stripping."

[168] *In re* Guantanamo Cases, 355 F. Supp. 2d 443 (D.D.C. 2005) and Khalid v. Bush, 355 F. Supp. 2d 311 (D.D.C. 2005), *consolidated, vacated and dismissed sub nom.* Boumediene v. Bush, 476 F.3d 981 (D.C. Cir. 2007).

[169] Al Odah v. United States, 321 F.3d 1134 (D.C. Cir 2003), ***rev'd sub nom*** Rasul v. Bush, 542 U.S. 466 (2004).

[170] 339 U.S. 763 (1950).

[171] 476 F.3d 981 (D.C. Cir. 2007). Judge Randolph, joined by Judge Sentelle, found that the measure does not constitute a suspension of the Writ within the meaning of the Constitution because the majority was "aware of no case prior to 1789 going the detainees' way," and were thus convinced that "the writ in 1789 would not have been available to aliens held at an overseas military base leased from a foreign government." Judge Rogers, in dissent, would have given greater deference to the Supreme Court's *Rasul* opinion, in which it drew a distinction between the situation faced by the Guantanamo detainees and the post-WWII convicts, 542 U.S. 466, 475 (2004), and in which it found the naval base to be within the historical scope of the Writ. *Boumediene*, 476 F.3d at 1002 (Rogers, J., dissenting))(citing Sierra Club v. EPA, 322 F.3d 718, 724 (D.C. Cir. 2003)).

[172] Boumediene v. Bush, 127 S.Ct. 1478 (2007).

[173] Justice Stevens, joined by Justice Kennedy, wrote a statement explaining their view that, "despite the obvious importance of the issues raised," the petitioners should first exhaust remedies available under the DTA unless the petitoners can show that the government is causing delay or some other ongoing injury that would make those remedies inadequate. *Id.* at 1478. Justice Breyer, joined by Justices Souter and Ginsburg, would have granted certiorari to provide immediate attention to the issues. The dissenters viewed it as unlikely that further treatment by the lower courts might elucidate the issues, given that the MCA limits jurisdiction to the Court of Appeals for the D.C. Circuit, which had already indicated that Guantanamo detainees have no constitutional rights. Justices Breyer and Souter would have granted expedited consideration.

[174] U.S. CONST. Art. 1, § 9, cl. 2.

[175] *Boumediene* at 2248 (citing INS v. St. Cyr, 533 U. S. 289, 300 — 301(2001)).

[176] *Id.* at 2247.

[177] *Id.* at 2253.

[178] *Id.* at 2258.

[179] *See* De Lima v. Bidwell, 182 U. S. 1 (1901); Dooley v. United States, 182 U. S. 222 (1901); Armstrong v. United States, 182 U. S. 243 (1901); Downes v. Bidwell, 182 U. S. 244; Hawaii v. Mankichi, 190 U. S. 197 (1903); Dorr v. United States, 195 U. S. 138 (1904).

[180] *Boumediene*, at 2255-56, 2258 (discussing plurality opinion in Reid v. Covert, 354 U. S.1 (1957)). In his concurring opinion in *Reid*, Justice Harlan argued that whether a constitutional provision has extraterritorial effect depends upon the "particular circumstances, the practical necessities, and the possible alternatives which Congress had before it" and, in particular, whether judicial enforcement of the provision would be "impracticable and anomalous." *Reid*, 354 U.S. at 74 — 75 (Harlan, J., concurring in result).

[181] *Id.* at 2260.

[182] *Id.* at 2262.

[183] *Boumediene*, at 2266-67.

[184] *Id.* at 2268.

[185] *Id.* at 2269.

[186] *Id.* at 2270.

[187] *Id.*

[188] *Id.* at 2275.

[189] *See Boumediene*, at 2274 ("In view of our holding we need not discuss the reach of the writ with respect to claims of unlawful conditions of treatment or confinement.").

[190] *Id.* at 2275.

[191] U.S. Dist. Court for the District of Columbia, Resolution of the Executive Session, July 1, 2008, available at [http://www.dcd.uscourts.gov/public-docs/system/files/Guantanamo-Resolution070108.pdf].

[192] For a general background and description of related writs, see 39 AM. JUR. 2d. *HabeasCorpus* § 1 (1999).

[193] *See generally* S. DOC. NO. 108-17 at 848 *et seq.*

[194] Rasul v. Bush, 542 U.S. 466 (2004).

[195] *Ex parte* Watkins, 28 U.S. (3 Pet.) 193, 201 (1830) (Marshall, C.J.) ("The writ of habeascorpus is a high prerogative writ, known to the common law, the great object of which is theliberation of those who may be imprisoned without sufficient cause.").

[196] 39 AM. JUR. 2d. *Habeas Corpus* § 27 (1999).

[197] *Ex parte* Bollman, 8 U.S. (4 Cr.) 75 (1807).

[198] *Id.* at 94.

[199] Immigration and Naturalization Service v. St. Cyr, 533 U.S. 289, 301 (U.S. 2001).

[200] Felker v. Tupin, 518 U.S. 663 (1996)(citing Swain v. Pressley, 430 U.S. 372 (1977)).

[201] See *Boumediene* at 2248 (" The Court has been careful not to foreclose the possibility that the protections of the Suspension Clause have expanded along with post-1789 developments that define the present scope of the writ.").

[202] *Cf.* INS v. St. Cyr, 533 U.S. 289, 340 n.5 (2001) (Scalia, J., dissenting)("If . . . the writ could not be suspended within the meaning of the Suspension Clause until Congress affirmatively provided for habeas by statute, then surely Congress may subsequently alter what it had initially provided for, lest the Clause become a one-way ratchet.").

[203] *Cf. Felker* (Holding that restrictions on successive petitions for *habeas corpus* by prisoners convicted in state courts did not suspend the writ, but merely applied a modified *res judicata* rule to control abuse of the writ); *Boumediene* at 2276-77 (explaining that some reasonable regulations on *habeas* cases to relieve governmental burden or preservesecurity will be permissible).

[204] *See* United States v. Hayman, 342 U.S. 205 (1952); Hill v. United States, 368 U.S. 424 (1962); Swain v. Pressley, 430 U.S. 372 (1977); Felker v. Turpin, 518 U.S. 651 (1996); Immigration and Naturalization Service v. St. Cyr, 533 U.S. 289 (2001).

[205] *Boumediene* at 2266.

[206] The *Boumediene* Court did not address the matter because the MCA did not purport to act as a formal suspension of the writ. *Boumediene* at 2262.

[207] The Attorney General's prepared statement is available at [http://www.scotusblog. com/wp/ mukasey-curb-courts-powers-on-detainees/].

[208] See Improving Detainee Policy: Handling Terrorism Detainees within the American Justice System, Hearing before the Senate Judiciary Committee, June 4, 2008. For a review and criticism of some proposals, see the Constitution Project, *A Critique of "National Security Courts,"* available at [http://www.constitutionproject.org/pdf/Critique_of_the_National_Security_Courts.pdf].

[209] *See, e.g.*, 18 U.S.C. § 2332 (prescribing penalties for homicides of U.S. nationals abroad and other violence directed at the United States, so long as the act is "intended to coerce, intimidate, or retaliate against a government or a civilian population"); 18 U.S.C. § 2232b (acts of terrorism transcending national boundaries).

[210] *See* 18 U.S.C. § 2339B (provision of material support to designated terrorist organization prior to amendment by P.L. 108-458, § 6603(d), December 17, 2004); *see also* 18 U.S.C. § 2339 (proscribing harboring or concealing terrorists, but only after October 26, 2001 enactment of P.L. 107-56, title VIII, § 803(a)). The *Ex Post Facto* Clause prevents prosecution for charges that would not have been applicable when the offense occurred, U.S. CONST. art. 1, § 9, cl. 3.

[211] *Boumediene*, at 67.

[212] See *Boumediene*, at 37-38, 54-56.

[213] 486 U.S. at 612-13 (Scalia, J., dissenting).

[214] Bartlett v. Bowen, 816 F.2d 695, 719-720 (1987)(Bork, J., dissenting).

[215] *See e.g.*, First English Evangelical Lutheran Church of Glendale v. Los Angeles County, 482 U.S. 304 (1987)(holding that the Constitution mandates effective remedies for takings).

[216] *See* Gov't Br. Address. Pend. Prelim. Mots. at 49-51, Bismullah v. Gates, No. 06-1197 (D.C. Cir.).

[217] Bismullah v. Gates, No. 06-1197 (D.C. Cir. July 20, 2007)(order on procedural motions).

[218] *See* DOD Press Release, "DoD Announces Draft Detainee Review Policy" (March 3, 2004), *available at* [http://www.defenselink.mil/releases/2004/nr20040303-0403.html]; Memorandum from Deputy Secretary of Defense, Revised Implementation of Administrative Review Procedures for Enemy Combatants Detained at U.S. Navy Base, Guantanamo Bay, Cuba (July 14, 2006), *available at* [http://www.defenselink.mil/news/Aug2006/d20060809ARBProceduresMemo.pdf].

[219] CSRT Implementing Directive, *supra* note 28, at encl. 10 (implementing Detainee Treatment Act provisions).

[220] *Boumediene* at 2273-74 (stating that the ability to request a new CSRT to consider new evidence is an "insufficient replacement for the factual review these detainees are entitled to receive through habeas corpus").

[221] "A motion pursuant to § 2241 generally challenges the execution of a federal prisoner's sentence, including such matters as the administration of parole, computation of a prisoner's sentence by prison officials, prison disciplinary actions, prison transfers, type of detention and prison conditions." Jiminian v. Nash, 245 F.3d 144 (2d Cir. 2001). *See, e.g.*, Rickenbacker v. United States, 365 F. Supp. 2d 347 (E.D.N.Y. 2005) (challenging failure to provide drug and psychiatric treatment in accordance with sentencing court's recommendation).

[222] 28 U.S.C. § 1331. *See* Caldwell v. Miller, 790 F.2d 589 (7th Cir. 1986).

[223] Russell Donaldson, *Mandamus, under 28 U.S.C.A. §1361, To Obtain Change in Prison Condition or Release of Federal Prisoner*, 114 A.L.R. Fed. 225 (2005). Relief in mandamus is generally available where: (1) the plaintiff can showa clear legal right to the performance of the requested action; (2) the duty of the official in question is clearly defined and nondiscretionary; (3) there is no other adequate remedy available to the plaintiff; (4) there are other separate jurisdictional grounds for the action. *Id.* at 1(a). A writ of mandamus may issue only where "the duty to be performed is ministerial and the obligation to act peremptory, and clearly defined. The law must not only authorize the demanded action, but require it; the duty must be clear and undisputable." Ali v. Ashcroft, 350 F. Supp. 2d 28, 65 (D.D.C. 2004), *quoting* Shoshone-Bannock Tribes v. Reno, 56 F.3d 1476, 1479 (D.C. Cir. 1995).

[224] *See* Long v. Parker, 390 F.2d. 816 (3rd Cir. 1968) (prisoner suit to obtain access to religious weekly newspaper stated a valid cause of action worthy of a factual hearing).

[225] Stover v. Carlson, 413 F. Supp. 718 (D. Conn. 1976) (ending federal prison practice of opening privileged communications outside of prisoner's presence).

[226] Fullwood v. Clemmer, 206 F. Supp. 370 (D.D.C. 1962) (keeping prisoner in solitary confinement for more than two years for minor disciplinary infractions violates the Eighth Amendment). It should be noted that where a prisoner has not yet been convicted of a crime, a challenge to conditions of detentions may sound in Due Process rather than as an Eighth Amendment challenge. Bell v. Wolfish, 441 U.S. 520 (1979).

[227] *See generally* Donaldson, *supra* note 220.

[228] See *Boumediene*, at 2274 ("In view of our holding we need not discuss the reach of the writ with respect to claims of unlawful conditions of treatment or confinement.").

[229] Paul Shukovsky, *Terrorism Suspect's Suit Tells of U.S. Abuse: Documents in Guantanamo Case Describe Extreme Isolation,* SEATTLE POST-INTELLIGENCER, August 6, 2004, at A1.

[230] Al-Anazi v. Bush, 370 F. Supp. 2d 188 (D.D.C. 2005).

[231] Josh White, *Lawyers Seek Improved Conditions for Suicidal Detainee*, WASH. POST, November 5, 2005, at A8.

[232] *See, e.g., In re* Guantanamo Detainee Cases, 355 F. Supp. 2d 443, 480-81 (D.D.C. 2005)(rejecting claims on other grounds).

[233] All Writs Act, 28 U.S.C. § 1651.

[234] Belbach v. Bush, 520 F.3d 452, 456 (D.C. Cir. 2008) (holding the MCA leaves intact the presumptive jurisdiction of federal courts to inquire into the constitutionality of ajurisdiction-stripping statute).

[235] *See* El-Banna v. Bush, 2005 U.S. Dist. LEXIS 16880 (2005) (seeking preservation of records relating to treatment of detainees).

[236] Al-Anazi v. Bush, 370 F. Supp. 2d 188, 196 (D.D.C. 2005).

[237] 28 U.S.C. § 2243.

[238] Rules Governing § 2255 Cases, Rule 7, 28 U.S.C.A. foll. § 2255 (applicable to prisoners subject to sentence of a federal court).

[239] 28 U.S.C. § 2243.

[240] 28 U.S.C. § 2255.

[241] CSRT Implementing Directive, *supra* note 28, at encl. 1, para. I(9)-(10).

[242] *See* Mark Denbeaux *et al., No-Hearing Hearings, CSRT: The Modern Habeas Corpus?*, at 37-40 (2006), *available at* [http://law.shu.edu/news/final_no_hearing_hearings_report. pdf]. The named author is a professor at Seton Hall University School of Law and serves as counsel to two Guantanamo detainees.

[243] *Boumediene* at 2271.

[244] *See* Gov't Br. in Opp. to Pet. for Reh'g, Boumediene v. Bush, No. 16-1195 (U.S.).

[245] *See, e.g.*, Landon v. Plasencia, 459 U.S. 21, 32 (1981) ("This Court has long held that an alien seeking initial admission to the United States requests a privilege and has no constitutional rights regarding his application, for the power to admit or exclude aliens is a sovereign prerogative"); Shaughnessy v. United States *ex rel.* Mezei, 345 U.S. 206, 216 (1953) (finding that an inadmissible alien's "right to enter the United States depends on the congressional will, and courts cannot substitute their judgment for the legislative mandate"). On the other hand, whether or not a *habeas* court would ever deem the release into the United States of an alien with no prior ties to the country as an appropriate remedy to his unlawful detention abroad remains uncertain. At least one Guantanamo detainee has requested a federal district court to order the government to parole him into the United States pending resolution of his habeas claim. Husaifa Parhat's Motion for Immediate Release on Parole into the Continental United States Pending Final Judgment on His Habeas Petition, In re: Guantanamo Bay Litigation, No. 05-1509 (July 23, 2008).

[246] *Boumediene* at 2261-62.

[247] *See* Khadr v. United States, No. 07-1405 (D.C. Cir. June 20, 2008); Hamdan v. Gates, No. 04-1519 (JR) (D.D.C. July 18, 2008)(order denying injunction of military commission proceedings).

[248] *See ex parte* Milligan, 71 U.S. (4 Wall.) 2, 115-16 (1866); *cf. ex parte* Quirin, 317 U.S. 1, 24-25 (1942)(dismissing contention that presidential proclamation stripped Court of authority to review case, stating that "nothing in the Proclamation precludes access to the courts for determining its applicability to the particular case").

[249] Schlesinger v. Councilman, 420 U.S. 738, 759 (1975)(finding judicial abstention is not appropriate in cases in which individuals raise " 'substantial arguments denying the right of the military to try them at all,' " and in which the legal challenge "turn[s] on the status of the persons as to whom the military asserted its power"); United States *ex rel.* Toth v. Quarles, 350 U.S. 11, 76 (1955).

[250] *Cf.* New v. Cohen, 129 F.3d 639, 643 (D.C. Cir. 1997).

[251] The latter part of this quoted language dovetails with clause 9 of § 8 of Article I, under which Congress is authorized "[t]o constitute tribunals inferior to the supreme Court."

[252] Although the position of Chief Justice is not specifically mandated, it is referenced in Article I, § 3, Cl. 6, in connection with the procedure for the Senate impeachment trial of a President:

The Senate shall have the sole Power to try all Impeachments. When sitting for that Purpose, they shall be on oath or affirmation. When the President of the United States is tried, the Chief Justice shall preside: and no Person shall be convicted without Concurrence of two-thirds of the Members present.

[253] By the Judiciary Act of 1789, it was established that the Court was to be composed of the Chief Justice and five Associate Justices. The number of Justices was gradually increased to ten, until in 1869 the number was fixed at nine, where it has remained to this day.

[254] 28 U.S.C. §§ 81-131, 132.

[255] 28 U.S.C. §§ 41, 43 (District of Columbia Circuit, First Circuit through Eleventh Circuit, Federal Circuit).

[256] *See, e.g.*, 28 U.S.C. §§ 151 (U.S. bankruptcy courts); 251 (U.S. Court of International Trade).

[257] Williams v. Rhodes, 393 U.S. 23, 29 (1968).

[258] United States v. Bitty, 208 U.S. 393, 399-400 (1908).

[259] Laurence Tribe, *Jurisdictional Gerrymandering: Zoning Disfavored Rights Out of the Federal Courts*, 16 HARV. C.R.-C.L.L. REV. 129, 142-43 (1981). For instance, segregation in courtrooms is unlawful and may not be enforced through contempt citations for disobedience, Johnson v. Virginia, 373 U.S. 61 (1963), or through other means. Treatment of parties to or witnesses in judicial actions based on their race is impermissible. Hamilton v. Alabama, 376 U.S. 650 (1964)(reversing contempt conviction of witness who refused to answer questions so long as prosecutor addressed her by her first name).

[260] The Fifth Amendment provides that no "private property [ ] be taken for public use without just compensation."

[261] 424 U.S. 1, 109-43 (1976).

[262] It is true that the Court has wavered between two approaches to cases raising separation-of-powers claims, using a strict approach in some cases and a less rigid balancing approach in others. Nevertheless, the Court looks to a test that evaluates whether the moving party, usually Congress, has "impermissibly undermine[d]" the power of another branch or has "impermissibly aggrandize[d]" its own power at the expense of another branch; whether, that is, the moving party has "disrupt[ed] the proper balance between the coordinate branches [by] preventing the [other] Branch from accomplishing itsconstitutionally assigned functions." Morrison v. Olson, 487 U.S. 654, 695 (1988). *See also*INS v. Chadha, 462 U.S. 919 (1983); Bowsher v. Synar, 478 U.S. 714 (1986); Mistretta v.United States, 488 U.S. 361 (1989); Metropolitan Washington Airports Auth. v. Citizens forthe Abatement of Airport Noise, 501 U.S. 252 (1991).

[263] *Boumediene* at 2259(calling the writ of habeas corpus "an indispensable mechanism formonitoring the separation of powers").

[264] 2 U.S. (2 Dall.) 409 (1792). This case was not actually decided by the Supreme Court,but by several Justices on circuit.

[265] Those principles remain vital. *See, e.g.*, Chicago & S. Air Lines v. Waterman S. S. Corp.,333 U.S. 103, 113-14 (1948)("Judgments within the powers vested in courts by the JudiciaryArticle of the Constitution may not lawfully be revised, overturned or refused faith andcredit by another Department of Government."); Connor v. Johnson, 402 U.S. 690 (1971).

[266] Northern Pipeline Constr. Co. v. Marathon Pipe Line Co., 458 U.S. 50 (1982).

[267] S.Rept. 110-90.

[268] S.Amdt. 2022 to S.Amdt. 2011 to H.R. 1585, 153 CONG. REC. S11559 (daily ed. July 19, 2007).Chapter 3

In: Closing Guantanamo - Issues and Legal... ISBN: 978-1-60741-511-4
Editor: Noah M. Claeys

Chapter 3

BOUMEDIENE V. BUSH: GUANTANAMO DETAINEES' RIGHT TO *HABEAS CORPUS*[*]

Michael John Garcia

SUMMARY

In the consolidated cases of *Boumediene v. Bush* and *Al Odah v. United States*, decided June 12, 2008, the Supreme Court held in a 5-4 opinion that aliens designated as enemy combatants and detained at the U.S. Naval Station in Guantanamo Bay, Cuba, have the constitutional privilege of *habeas corpus*. The Court also found that § 7 of the Military Commissions Act (MCA), which limited judicial review of executive determinations of the petitioners' enemy combatant status, did not provide an adequate *habeas* substitute and therefore acted as an unconstitutional suspension of the writ of *habeas*. The immediate impact of the *Boumediene* decision is that detainees at Guantanamo may petition a federal district court for *habeas* review of the circumstances of their detention. This report summarizes the *Boumediene* decision and analyzes several of its major implications for the U.S. detention of alien enemy combatants and legislation that limits detainees' access to judicial review. For discussion of litigation challenging detention policy, see CRS Report RL33180, *Enemy Combatant Detainees: Habeas Corpus Challenges in*

[*] This is an edited, reformatted and augmented version of a CRS Report for Congress publication dated September 2008.

Federal Court, by Jennifer K. Elsea, Michael John Garcia, and Kenneth R. Thomas.

In the consolidated cases of *Boumediene v. Bush* and *Al Odah v. United States*,[1] decided June 12, 2008, the Supreme Court held in a 5-4 opinion that aliens designated as enemy combatants and detained at the U.S. Naval Station in Guantanamo Bay, Cuba, have the constitutional privilege of *habeas corpus*. The Court also found that § 7 of the Military Commissions Act (MCA),[2] which limited judicial review of executive determinations of the petitioners' enemy combatant status, did not provide an adequate *habeas* substitute and therefore acted as an unconstitutional suspension of the writ of *habeas*. The immediate impact of the *Boumediene* decision is that detainees at Guantanamo may petition a federal district court for *habeas* review of the circumstances of their detention.

BACKGROUND

Following the terrorist attacks of 9/11, Congress passed the Authorization to Use Military Force (AUMF), which authorized the President "to use all necessary and appropriate force against those ... [who]planned, authorized, committed, or aided the terrorist attacks" against the United States."[3] As part of the subsequent "war on terror," many persons captured during military operations in Afghanistan and elsewhere were transferred to the U.S. Naval Station in Guantanamo Bay, Cuba, for detention and possible prosecution for war crimes. In the 2004 case of *Hamdi v. Rumsfeld*, a majority of the Supreme Court recognized that, as a necessary incident to theAUMF,thePresident was authorized to detain persons captured whilefighting U.S. forces in Afghanistan for the duration of the conflict.[4] The Department of Defense thereafter established Combatant Status Review Tribunals (CSRTs) to assess whether persons detained at Guantanamo constituted "enemy combatants" who could be detained for the duration of the "war on terror" and prosecuted in military commissions for any war crimes committed.

On the same day that *Hamdi* was decided, the Court issued an opinion in the case of *Rasul v. Bush*,[5] holding that the federal *habeas* statute, 28 U.S.C. § 2241, extended statutory *habeas* jurisdiction with respect to persons held in Guantanamo. Immediately thereafter, dozens of *habeas* petitions were filed on behalf of Guantanamo detainees in the U.S. District Court for the District of Columbia (District Court), where judges reached conflicting conclusions as to whether the detainees had any enforceable rights to challenge their treatment and detention.

Shortly after the Supreme Court granted certiorari to hear a challenge by one of the detainees to his trial by military tribunal, Congress passed the Detainee Treatment Act of 2005 (DTA).[6] The DTA divested the courts of jurisdiction to hear challenges by Guantanamo detainees based on their treatment or living conditions, and eliminated federal courts' jurisdiction under 28 U.S.C. § 2241 to consider *habeas* claims by aliens challenging their detention at Guantanamo. The DTA provided the U.S. Court of Appeals for the D.C. Circuit (D.C. Circuit) with exclusive jurisdiction to review detainee status determinations made by CSRTs or military commissions. In the 2006 case of *Hamdan v. Rumsfeld*,[7] the Court interpreted these provisions as being inapplicable to *habeas* cases pending at the time the DTA was enacted. In response, Congress passed the MCA, which amended the federal *habeas* statute to expressly eliminate court jurisdiction over all pending and future causes of action, other than pursuant to the limited review permitted under the DTA.

The petitioners in *Boumediene* are aliens detained at Guantanamo who sought *habeas* review of their continued detention and designation as enemy combatants by CSRTs in District Court. On appeal, the D.C. Circuit held that the MCA stripped it and all other federal courts of jurisdiction to consider petitioners' *habeas* applications. Relying upon its earlier opinion in *Al Odah v. United States* and the 1950 Supreme Court case *Johnson v. Eisentrager*,[8] in which the Supreme Court found that the constitutional writ of *habeas* did not apply to enemy aliens detained in post-WWII Germany, the D.C. Circuit held that the MCA's "court-stripping"[9] provision did not operate as an unconstitutional suspension of the writ, because aliens held by the U.S. in foreign territory do not have a constitutional right to *habeas*.[10]

Although the Supreme Court initiallydenied the petitioners' request for review, it subsequently reversed itself and granted certiorari in June 2007 to consider the consolidated cases of *Boumediene* and *Al Odah*. In an opinion by Justice Kennedy that was joined byJustices Breyer, Ginsburg, Souter, and Stevens, the Court reversed the D.C. Circuit and held thatpetitioners had a constitutional right to *habeas* that was withdrawn by the MCA in violation of the Constitution's Suspension Clause.[11] Chief Justice Roberts and Justice Scalia wrote separate dissenting opinions, which were joined by the other and Justices Alito and Thomas. Justice Souter also wrote a brief concurring opinion, joined by Justices Breyer and Ginsburg, briefly disputing the dissenting opinions' purported characterization of the majority's decision.

APPLICATION OF MCA TO PENDING *HABEAS* ACTIONS

Before assessing petitioners' constitutional claims, the Court briefly addressed petitioners' argument that MCA § 7 did not deny federal courts jurisdiction to consider *habeas* actions likethoseof petitioners, which were pending at the time that the MCA was enacted. The Court rejected this argument, finding that the structure of MCA § 7 and the act's legislative history demonstrated that the MCA was intended to deprive federal courts of jurisdiction to consider *habeas* cases pending at the time of enactment.

CONSTITUTIONAL PRIVILEGE TO *HABEAS*

The Court next turned to the question of whether petitioners possess a constitutional privilege to seek the writ of *habeas corpus*. Petitioners argued that they possess a constitutional right to *habeas*, and that the MCA deprived them of this right in contravention of the Suspension Clause, which prohibits the suspension of the writ of *habeas* except "when in Cases of Rebellion or Invasion the public Safety may require it." The MCA did not expressly purport to be a formal suspension of the writ of *habeas*, and the government did not make such a claim to the Court. Instead, the government argued that aliens designated as enemy combatants and detained outside the *de jure* territory of the United States have no constitutional rights, including the constitutional privilege to *habeas*, and that therefore stripping the courts of jurisdiction to hear petitioners' *habeas* claims did not violate the Suspension Clause.

The Court began its analysis by surveying the history and origins of the writ of *habeas*, emphasizing the importance placed on the writ for the Framers. The Court noted that protection of the *habeas* privilege was one of the few safeguards to individual liberty contained in the Constitution prior to the addition of the Bill of Rights, and the Suspension Clause permits suspension of the writ only in the rare instance where public safety may require it as a result of invasion or rebellion. The Court characterized the Suspension Clause as not only a "vital instrument" for protecting individual liberty, but also a means to ensure that the judiciary branch would have, except in cases of formal suspension, "a time-tested device, the writ, to maintain the delicate balance of governance" between the branches and prevent "cyclical abuses" of the writ by the executive and legislative branches.[12] The Court stated that the separation-of-powers doctrine and the historyshapingthe design of the

Suspension Clause informed its interpretation of the reach and purpose of the Clause and the constitutional writ of *habeas*.

While the Court considered the history and function of the writ to be central to its analysis of the writ's application, it also sought guidance from founding-era authorities as to whether the constitutional writ of *habeas* was understood to cover foreign nationals apprehended and detained abroad during a time of serious threat to the country's security. While the Court cautioned that its jurisprudence had "been careful not to foreclose the possibility that the protections of the Suspension Clause have expanded along with post-1789 developments that define the present scope of the writ,"[13] at minimum the Clause would be deemed to protect the writ as it was recognized at the time the Constitution was drafted and ratified. The Court found the historical record to beinconclusivein resolving the issue before it, and suggested that "given the unique status of Guantanamo Bay and the particular dangers of terrorism in the modern age ... common-law courts simply may not have confronted cases with close parallels to this one."[14]

Nonetheless, the Court interpreted the Suspension Clause as having full effect at Guantanamo, rejecting the government's position that the Clause did not cover petitioners because the United States did not assert legal sovereignty over the territory where they were detained. While the Court did not question the government's position that Cuba maintains legal sovereignty over Guantanamo under the terms of the 1903 lease giving the U.S. plenary control over the territory, it disagreed with the government's position that "at least when applied to non-citizens, the Constitution necessarily stops where *de jure* sovereignty ends."[15]

Instead, the Court characterized its prior jurisprudence as recognizing that the Constitution's extraterritorial application turns on "objective factors and practical concerns."[16] Here, the Court emphasized the functional approach taken in the *Insular Cases*, where it had assessed the availability of constitutional rights in incorporated and unincorporated territories under the control of United States.[17] Although the government argued that the Court's subsequent decision in *Eisentrager* stood for the proposition that the constitutional writ of *habeas* does not extend to enemy aliens captured and detained abroad, the Court found this reading to be overly constrained. According to theCourt, interpreting the *Eisentrager* ruling in this formalistic manner would be inconsistent with the functional approach taken by the Court in other cases concerning the Constitution's extraterritorial application,[18] and would disregard the practical considerations that informed the *Eisentrager* Court's decision that the petitioners were precluded from seeking *habeas*.

The Court also found that accepting the government's sovereignty-based approach to the Constitution's applicability would raise significant separation-of-powers concerns, as the political branches would be free "to govern without legal constraint" in a territory like Guantanamo, where the U.S. disclaimed legal sovereignty but exercised plenary control:

> The Constitution grants Congress and the President the power to acquire, dispose of, and govern territory, not the power to decide when and where its terms may apply. Even when the United States acts outside its borders, its powers are not absolute and unlimited but are subject to such restrictions as are expressed in the Constitution.... To hold that the political branches may switch the Constitution on and off at will would lead to a regime where they, not this Court, say what the law is.... These concerns have particular bearing upon the Suspension Clause ... for the writ is itself an indispensable mechanism for monitoring the separation of powers. The test for determining the scope of this provision must not be subject to manipulation by those whose power it is designed to restrain.[19]

Based on the language found in the *Eisentrager* decision and other cases concerning the extraterritorial application of the Constitution, the Court deemed at least three factors to be relevant in assessing the extraterritorial scope of the Suspension Clause: (1) the citizenship and status of the detainee and the adequacy of the status determination process; (2) the nature of the site where the person is seized and detained; and (3) practical obstacles inherent in resolving the prisoner's entitlement to the writ.

Applying this framework, the Court characterized petitioners' circumstances in the instant case as being significantly different from those of the detainees at issue in *Eisentrager*. Among other things, the Court noted that unlike the detainees in *Eisentrager*, the petitioners denied that they were enemy combatants, and the government's control of the post-WWII, occupied German territory in which the *Eisentrager* detainees were held was not nearly as significant nor secure as itscontrol over the territory where the petitioners are located. The Court also found that the procedural protections afforded to Guantanamo detainees in CSRT hearings are "far more limited [than those afforded to the *Eisentrager* detainees tried by military commission], and, we conclude, fall well short of the procedures and adversarial mechanisms that would eliminate the need for habeas corpus review."[20]

While acknowledging that it had never before held that noncitizens detained in another country's territory have any rights under the U.S. Constitution, the Court concluded that the case before it "lack[ed] any precise historical parallel."[21] In particular, the Court noted that the Guantanamo detainees have been held for the duration of a conflict that is already one of the longest in U.S. history, in territory that, while not technically part of the United States, is subject to complete U.S. control. Based on these factors, the Court concluded that the Suspension Clause has full effect at Guantanamo.

In a dissenting opinion joined by Chief Justice Roberts and Justices Alito and Thomas, Justice Scalia argued that the constitutional writ of *habeas* "does not, and never has, run in favor of aliens abroad; the Suspension Clause thus has no application, and the Court's intervention in this military matter is entirely *ultra vires*."[22] Justice Scalia further argued that the judiciary is ill-equipped to address the national security concerns raised by the detention of enemy combatants. According to the dissent, the procedural and evidentiary rules likely to be employed by the judiciary in reviewing a detainee's status would increase the likelihood that enemy combatants would mistakenly be released back into hostilities.

In a concurring opinion joined by Justices Breyer and Ginsburg, Justice Souter claimed that the Court's interpretation of the extraterritorial scope of the constitutional writ of *habeas* was not nearly as surprising as Justice Scalia's dissent suggested, given Court dictum in *Rasul v. Bush* stating that "[a]pplication of the habeas statute to persons detained at [Guantanamo] is consistent with the historical reach of the writ of habeas corpus."[23]

ADEQUACY OF *HABEAS CORPUS* SUBSTITUTE

Having decided that petitioners possessed a constitutional privilege to *habeas corpus*, the Court next assessed whether the court-stripping measure of MCA § 7 was impermissible under the Suspension Clause. Because the MCA did not purport to be a formal suspension of the writ, the question before the Court was whether Congress had provided an adequate substitute for *habeas corpus*. The government argued that the MCA complied with the Suspension Clause because it applied the DTA's review process to petitioners, which the government claimed was a constitutionally adequate *habeas* substitute.

Because the D.C. Circuit had found that the constitutional writ of *habeas* did not run to petitioners, it did not consider whether an adequate substitute was provided. While the Court noted that it generally remands cases back to the lower court for consideration of issues not addressed in the first instance, it found that the "exceptional" circumstances of the present case — including the separation-of-powers issues it raised and the fact that petitioners had been denied meaningful access to a judicial forum for a number of years — warranted a departure from ordinary practice. The Court also noted that an interim order by a three-judge D.C. Circuit panel in the case of *Bismullah v. Gates*[24] provided it with guidance as to the appellate court's construction of key DTA provisions.

The Court found its prior rulings addressing the adequacy of *habeas* substitutes enacted by Congress provided little guidance in assessing the adequacy of the jurisdiction-stripping provisions of the MCA and DTA. Prior congressional enactments typically attempted to streamline rather than circumscribe *habeas* review. In contrast, the intent of the MCA and DTA was to establish a more limited review procedure than *habeas*, as evidenced by, *inter alia*, the MCA's unequivocal jurisdiction-stripping language; the legislative history of both enactments; a comparison of the review permitted by the DTA and the unamended federal *habeas* statute; and the lack of a savings provision under either the DTA or MCA preserving *habeas* review as an avenue of last resort.

Though the Court declined to "offer a comprehensive summary of the requisites for an adequate substitute for *habeas corpus*," it nonetheless deemed the *habeas* privilege, at minimum, as entitling a prisoner "to a meaningful opportunity to demonstrate that he is being held pursuant to 'the erroneous application or interpretation' of relevant law," and empowering a court "to order the conditional release of an individual unlawfully detained," though release need not be the exclusive remedy or appropriate in every instance where the writ is granted.[25] Additionally, the necessary scope of *habeas* review may be broader, depending upon "the rigor of any earlier proceedings."[26]

The Court noted that petitioners identified numerous alleged deficiencies in the CSRT process which limited a detainee's ability to present evidence rebutting the government's claim that he is an enemy combatant. Among other things, cited deficiencies include constraints upon the detainee's ability to find and present evidence atthe CSRT stage to challenge the government's case; the failure toprovide a detainee with assistance of counsel; limiting the detainee's access to government records other than those that are unclassified, potentiallyresultingin adetaineebeing unaware of critical allegations relied upon by the government to order his detention; and the fact that thedetainee's abilityto confront witnesses may be "more theoretical than real,"[27] given the minimal limitations placed upon the admission of hearsay evidence.

While the Court did not determine whether theCSRTs, aspresently constituted, satisfy due process standards, it agreed with petitioners that there was "considerable risk of error in the tribunal's findings of fact."[28] "[G]iven that the consequence of error may be detention for the duration of hostilities that may last a generation or more, this is a risk too serious to ignore."[29] The Court held that for either the writ of *habeas* or an adequate substitute to function as an effective remedy for petitioners, a court conducting a collateral proceeding must have the ability to (1) correct errors in the CSRT process; (2) assess the sufficiency of the evidence against the detainee; and (3) admit and consider relevant exculpatory evidence that was not introduced in the prior proceeding.

The Court held that the DTA review process is a facially inadequate substitute for *habeas* review. It listed a number of potential constitutional infirmities in the review process, including the absence of provisions (1) empowering the D.C. Circuit to order release from detention; (2) permitting petitioners to challenge the President's authority to detain them indefinitely; (3) enabling the appellate court to review or correct the CSRT's findings of fact; and (4) permitting the detainee to present exculpatory evidence discovered after the conclusion of CSRT proceedings. The Court declined to read into the DTA each of the necessary procedures identified. As a result, the Court deemed MCA §7's application of the DTA review process to petitioners asfailingto provide an adequate substitute for *habeas*, therefore effecting an unconstitutional suspension of the writ.

In light of this conclusion, the Court held that petitioners could immediately pursue *habeas* review in federal district court, without first obtaining review of their CSRT designations from the D.C. Circuit as would otherwise be required under the DTA review process. While prior jurisprudence recognized that prisoners are generally required to exhaust alternative remedies before seeking federal *habeas* relief, the Court found that petitioners in the instant case were entitled to a prompt *habeas* hearing, given the fact that they had been detained for years without access to judicial oversight to which they were constitutionally privileged. The Court stressed, however, that except in cases ofundue delay, federal courts should generally refrain from considering *habeas* petitions of detainees being held as enemy combatants until after the CSRT had an opportunity to review their status. Acknowledging that the government possesses a "legitimate interest in protecting sources and methods of intelligence gathering," the Court announced that it expected courts reviewing Guantanamo detainees *habeas* claims to use "discretion to accommodatethisinteresttothe greatest extent possible," so as toavoid "widespread dissemination of classified information."[30]

In a dissenting opinion, Chief Justice Roberts — joined by Justices Alito, Thomas, and Scalia — argued that the DTA review process adequately protects any constitutional rights that aliens detained abroad as enemy combatants mayenjoy,and criticized the majority for replacing the DTA review system with "a set of shapeless procedures to be defined by federal courts at some future date."[31] Chief Justice Roberts argued that the Court should not have granted certiorari to review petitioners' claims until the D.C. Circuit had the opportunity to assess whether the remedies available under the DTA review process vindicated whatever constitutional and statutory rights petitioners' may possess. In a concurring opinion, Justice Souter argued that the dissenting justices' criticism of the majority's decision to permit detainees to immediate petition for *habeas* failed to sufficiently considertheduration that petitioners' had been denied meaningful judicial review of their claims.

IMPLICATIONS OF *BOUMEDIENE*

As a result of the *Boumediene* decision, detainees currentlyheld at Guantanamo may petition a federal district court for *habeas* review of status determinations made by a CSRT. However, the full consequences of the *Boumediene* decision are likely to be significantly broader. While the petitioners in *Boumediene* sought *habeas* review of their designation as enemy combatants, the Court's ruling that the constitutional writ of *habeas* extends to Guantanamo suggests that detainees may also seek judicial review of claims concerning unlawful conditions of treatment or confinement or to protest a planned transfer to the custody of another country.[32]

Some 250 *habeas* petitions have been filed on behalf of Guantanamo detainees in the U.S. District Court for the District of Columbia. In the aftermath of the *Boumediene* ruling, the District Court adopted a resolution for the coordination and management of Guantanamo cases. The resolution calls for all current and future Guantanamo cases to be transferred by the judge to whom they have been assigned to Senior Judge Thomas F. Hogan, who has been designated to coordinate and manage all Guantanamo cases so that they could be "addressed as expeditiously as possible as required bythe Supreme Court in *Boumedienev. Bush....*"[33] Judge Hogan is responsible for identifying and ruling on procedural issues common to the cases. The transferring judge will retain the case for all other purposes, though Judge Hogan is to confer with those judges whose cases raise common substantive issues, and he may address those issues with the consent of the transferring judge. District Court Judges Richard J. Leon and Emmet G. Sullivan have declined to transfer their cases for coordination, and it is possible that the three judges may reach differing opinions regarding issues common to their respective cases.

The conduct of trials before military commissions at Guantanamo may also be affected by *Boumediene*, as enemy combatants may now potentially raise constitutional arguments against their trial and conviction. Aliens convicted of war crimes before military commissions may also potentially seek *habeas* review of their designation as an enemy combatant by the CSRT, a designation that served as a legal requisite for their subsequent prosecution before a military commission.

Although the *Boumediene* Court held that DTA review procedures were an inadequate substitute for *habeas*, it expressly declined to assess "the content of the law that governs" the detention of aliens at Guantanamo.[34] The majority opinion noted that it made "no judgment as to whether the CSRTs, as currently constituted, satisfy due process standards," and emphasized that "both the DTA and the CSRT process remain intact."[35] Whether these procedures violate due process standards, facially or as applied in a given case, and whether a particular detainee is being unlawfully held, are issues to be addressed by the District Court when reviewing the *habeas* claims of Guantanamo detainees. Prior to the DTA and MCA's elimination of statutory jurisdiction over Guantanamo detainees' *habeas* claims, District Court judges reached inconsistent conclusions regarding the degree to which detainees could challenge their treatment and detention. In the aftermath of *Boumediene*, it is possible that continued disagreement between lower court judges concerning the scope of rights and remedies owed to Guantanamo detainees will eventually lead to a more definitive pronouncement by the Supreme Court.

Another question left unresolved in the Court's discussion of the extraterritorial application of the Constitution is the degree to which the writ of *habeas* and other constitutional protections apply to aliens detained in foreign locations other than Guantanamo (e.g., at military facilities in Afghanistan and elsewhere, or at any undisclosed U.S. detention sites overseas). The *Boumediene* Court indicated that it would take a functional approach in resolving such issues, taking into account "objective factors and practical concerns" in deciding whether the writ extended to aliens detained outside U.S. territory. Practical concerns mentioned in the majority's opinion as relevant to an assessment of the writ's extraterritorial application include the degree and likely duration of U.S. control over the location where the alien is held; the costs of holding the Suspension Clause applicable in a given situation, including the expenditure of funds to permit *habeas* proceedings and the likelihood that the proceedings would compromise or divert attention from a military mission; and the possibility that adjudicating a *habeas* petition would cause friction with the host government.[36] Interestingly, the *Boumediene* did not overrule the Court's prior decision in *Eisentrager*, in which it found that enemy detainees held in post-WWII Germanywere precluded from seeking *habeas* relief. Whether enemy aliens are held in conditions thatmorecloselyresemble those of the detainees at issuein *Eisentrager* or *Boumediene* may influence a reviewing court's assessment of whether they are owed the constitutional writ of *habeas*, as well as its assessment of the merits of any *habeas* claim deemed cognizable.

Although *Boumediene* deemed the limitations on judicial review imposed by the DTA and MCA to be an unconstitutional suspension of the writ of *habeas*, the Court did not foreclose all legislation altering the scope of review available in cases involving Guantanamo detainees. For example, the Court suggested that it would be a "legitimate objective" to channel all future cases involving Guantanamo detainees to one district court so as to reduce the administrative burdens upon the government.[37] The Court further acknowledged the government as having a legitimate interest in limiting the dissemination of classified intelligence-gathering information during the course of judicial hearings involving Guantanamo detainees. While the Court urged reviewing courts to use their discretion to protect this interest "to the greatest extent possible,"[38] some in Congress maywant to consider legislation to provide a statutory framework for the dissemination of classified information in cases involving Guantanamo detainees.

The Court's ruling in *Boumediene* did not necessarily bar all legislation that would limit judicial review of Guantanamo detainees' claims. Such legislation limiting judicial review a similar degree as the DTA or MCA might be deemed permissible if Congress also formally suspended the writ of *habeas* from being applied to Guantanamo detainees. It is far from certain, however, that a reviewing court would deem such legislation as compatible with Suspension Clause requirements. Assuming that the requirements of the Suspension Clause constituted a justiciable question, a reviewing court's assessment of the constitutionality of habeas-suspending legislation would likely turn on whether Al Qaeda's terrorist attacks upon the United States qualified as a "rebellion or invasion," and whether the court found that "the public safety" was therefore deemed to require the suspension of the writ in

Guantanamo, where a number of suspected Al Qaeda members and supporters are being detained.

Congress may still be able to impose some limitations upon judicial review of CSRT determinations if it strengthens the procedural protections afforded to detainees in CSRT status hearings. The Supreme Court identified a number of potential deficiencies in the status review process that necessitated *habeas* review of CSRT determinations, including the detainee's lack of counsel during the hearings; the presumption of validity accorded to the government's evidence; procedural and practical limitations upon the detainee's ability to present evidence rebutting the government's charges against him and to confront witnesses; potential limitations on the detainee's ability to introduce exculpatory evidence; and limitations on the detainee's ability to learn about the nature of the government's case against him to the extent that it is based upon classified evidence.[39] Legislation addressing some or all of these potential procedural inadequacies in the CSRT process might permit judicial review of CSRT determinations to be further streamlined.

For discussion of litigation challenging detention policy, see CRS Report RL33180, *Enemy Combatant Detainees: Habeas Corpus Challenges in Federal Court*, by Jennifer K. Elsea, Michael John Garcia, and Kenneth R. Thomas.

End Notes

[1] Boumediene v. Bush, 553 U.S. __, 128 S.Ct. 2229 (2008).
[2] P.L. 109-366 (2006).
[3] P.L. 107-40, 115 Stat. 224 (2001).
[4] Hamdi v. Rumsfeld, 542 U. S. 507, 518 (plurality opinion of O'Connor, J.); id. at 588-589 (Thomas, J., dissenting) (2004).
[5] 542 U.S. 466 (2004).
[6] P.L. 109-148, Title X (2005).
[7] 321 F.3d 1134 (D.C. Cir 2003), ***rev'd sub nom*** Rasul v. Bush, 542 U.S. 466 (2004).
[8] 339 U.S. 763 (1950).
[9] The practice of divesting courts of jurisdiction over particular issues is sometimes referred to as "court-stripping."
[10] 476 F.3d 981 (D.C. Cir. 2007).
[11] U.S. CONST. Art. 1, § 9, cl. 2.
[12] *Boumediene*, 128 S.Ct. at 2247.
[13] Id. at 2248 (citing INS v. St. Cyr, 533 U. S. 289, 300 — 301(2001)).
[14] Id. at 2251.
[15] Id. at 2253.
[16] Id. at 2258.

[17] See De Lima v. Bidwell, 182 U. S. 1 (1901); Dooley v. United States, 182 U. S. 222 (1901); Armstrong v. United States, 182 U. S. 243 (1901); Downes v. Bidwell, 182 U. S.244; Hawaii v. Mankichi, 190 U. S. 197 (1903); Dorr v. United States, 195 U. S. 138 (1904).

[18] *Boumediene*, 128 S.Ct. at 2255-2258 (discussing plurality opinion in Reid v. Covert, 354 U. S. 1 (1957)). In his concurring opinion in *Reid*, Justice Harlan argued that whether a constitutional provision has extraterritorial effect depends upon the "particular circumstances, the practical necessities, and the possible alternatives which Congress had before it" and, in particular, whether judicial enforcement of the provision would be "impracticable and anomalous." *Reid*, 354 U.S. at 74-75 (Harlan, J., concurring in result).

[19] *Boumediene*, 128 S.Ct. at 2259 (internal quotations omitted).

[20] Id. at 2260.

[21] Id. at 2262.

[22] *Boumediene*, 128 S.Ct. at 2294 (Scalia, J., dissenting).

[23] *Boumediene*, 128 S.Ct. at 2278 (Souter, J., concurring)(citing *Rasul*, 542 U.S. at 481).

[24] 501 F.3d 178 (D.C. Cir. 2007) (*Bismullah I*), ***reh'g denied***, 503 F.3d 137 (D.C. Cir. 2007) (*Bismullah II*); ***reh'g denied*** 514 F.3d 1291 (D.C. Cir. 2008)(*en banc*). On June 23, 2008, the Supreme Court granted certiorari and vacated the *Bismullah* decision, remanding the case back to the D.C. Circuit for reconsideration in light of the *Boumediene* decision. Gates v. Bismullah, 128 S.Ct. 2960 (2008). On August 22, 2008, the D.C. Circuit reinstated its decisions in *Bismullah I* and *Bismullah II*. Bismullah v. Gates, Case No. 06-1197, Order (D.C. Cir. August 22, 2008) (per curium), available at [http://www.scotusblog.com/wp/wp-content/uploads/2008/08/bismullah-order-8-22-08.pdf].

[25] *Boumediene*, 128 S.Ct. at 2265-2266.

[26] Id. at 2268.

[27] Id. at 2269.

[28] Id. at 2270.

[29] Id. at 2266.

[30] Id. at 2276.

[31] *Boumediene*, 128 S.Ct. at 2279 (Roberts, C.J., dissenting).

[32] See *Boumediene*, 128 S.Ct. at 2264 ("In view of our holdingwe need not discuss the reach of the writ with respect to claims of unlawful conditions of treatment or confinement.").

[33] U.S. Dist. Court for the District of Columbia, Resolution of the Executive Session, July 1, 2008, available at [http://www.dcd.uscourts.gov/publicocs/system/files/GuantanamoResolution070108.pdf].

[34] *Boumediene*, 128 S.Ct. at 2277.

[35] Id. at 2275.

[36] Id. at 2259-2262.

[37] Id. at 2276. Indeed, the Court suggested that legislation that amended the federal habeas statute might not be necessary to effectuate this measure; if a detainee files a *habeas* petition in another judicial district, the government can move for change of venue to the U.S. District Court for D.C. Id.

[38] Id.

[39] See *Boumediene*, 128 S.Ct. at 2260, 2269-2271.

INDEX

A

B

C

E

F

G

O

P

Q

R

S

Y